1 Introducing maps

1.1   What are maps?

We all use maps in our everyday lives. They help us find our way around. You have probably used a road map to help direct your parents from one place to another. You may have used a shopping centre plan such as the one in Figure 1 or a shop plan in order to find which floor a particular department is on.

Maps and plans show where things are in relation to one another. So, to be of any use, a map must contain accurate detail. Whenever you are making or reading a map, you should always be as detailed and accurate as possible.

Study Figure 2. It is a deck plan of a cross-channel ferry – the *Champs-Elysées*. Notice that the plan has a key containing a number of **symbols**. Symbols are an alternative to written labels and they save space. It is important to use clear and reasonably obvious symbols.

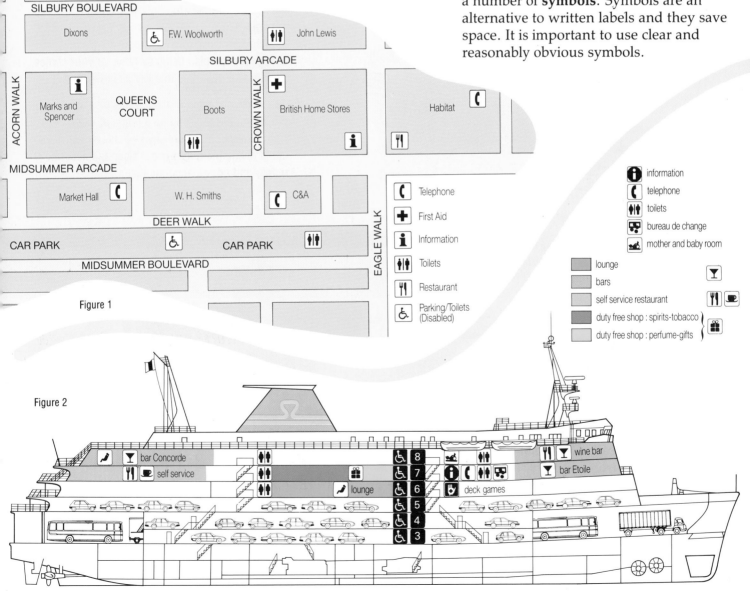

Figure 1

Telephone
First Aid
Information
Toilets
Restaurant
Parking/Toilets (Disabled)

information
telephone
toilets
bureau de change
mother and baby room

lounge
bars
self service restaurant
duty free shop : spirits-tobacco
duty free shop : perfume-gifts

Figure 2

bar Concorde
self service
lounge
deck games
wine bar
bar Etoile

Activities

1 Study Figure 2.
  a Which deck has only one set of toilets?
  b Which deck has a telephone?
  c Which deck has a mother and baby room?
  d Which deck has most bars?
  e From which deck can duty free goods be bought?
  f You get out of your car on deck 3 when a rather large and loud gentleman approaches you. He needs to get to the *Bar Etoile*. Use Figure 2 to give him detailed directions. Tell him what he will pass on his journey so that he knows he is on the right route.

  g Use Figure 2 to follow the route described:
    You have just eaten in the self-service restaurant. The ferry is rolling about and you are not feeling well, so you decide to take a walk. You walk towards the front of the ferry past some stairs. You see a sign saying **Duty Free Shop** *and you decide to take a look. After the duty free shop, you continue on the same deck and pass the* **Information Point.** *Feeling a little better, you go down the stairs one floor. You head away from the* **Lounge** *and enjoy the rest of the journey in the room just beyond the* **First Aid Point.** *What is the room?*

2 Figure 3 contains details of a re-arranged shop floor. You have been asked to produce a simple map using symbols to show where each department is now located. Your map will be put on display for customers. Produce a clear and colourful shop plan using symbols of your choice. Explain your symbols in a key as in Figure 2.

3 As a class collect and make a wall display of **maps** and **plans**. Build up a range of examples from newspapers, publicity leaflets, etc. You could divide them into two – clear and accurate maps, and poor inaccurate maps.

Emergency exit

Records Tapes C.D's

Electrical Household items

Cafeteria

Ladies toilet
Gents toilet

Ladies wear

Gents wear

Games Toys

Household goods and kitchenware

S T A I R S

Perfumes, Cosmetics Soaps

Gifts chocolates

Emergency exit

Figure 3

1.2   Mapping the local environment

It is very important for us to know about our own local environment before studying the geography of other places.

Figure 1 shows the route taken by Frances on her way to school. This type of sketch map is called a **mental map** as it has been drawn from memory. It has not been carefully surveyed in the way that most maps are. Notice she has drawn a number of important landmarks on her map. These would be helpful for anyone wanting to trace her route.

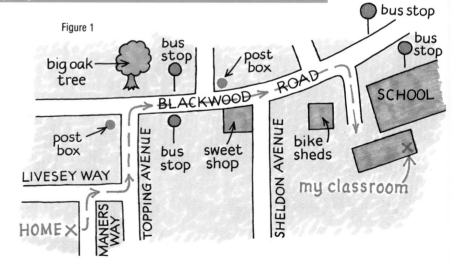

Figure 1

bus stop

bus stop

bus stop

big oak tree

bus stop

post box

BLACKWOOD ROAD

SCHOOL

post box

bus stop

sweet shop

bike sheds

my classroom

LIVESEY WAY

TOPPING AVENUE

SHELDON AVENUE

HOME ✗

MANERS WAY

EXPLORING GEOGRAPHY

1 The Local Environment and the UK

Simon Ross with Peter Eyre

Series editor Simon Ross

LONGMAN

Contents

1 Introducing maps — 1

1.1 What are maps? — 1
1.2 Mapping the local environment — 2
1.3 Understanding maps — 4
1.4 Using maps — 8
1.5 Using an altas — 10

2 Sense of place — 12

2.1 A sense of place in Britain — 12

3 Physical geography — 14

3.1 The physical geography of Britain — 14
3.2 Weathering — 15
3.3 Slopes — 17
3.4 Rivers — 18

4 Weather — 22

4.1 How the weather affects us — 22
4.2 Forecasting the weather — 23
4.3 The effect of buildings on local climate — 26
4.4 Measuring the weather — 28
4.5 Acid rain — 31

5 Resources and energy — 33

5.1 What is a resource? — 33
5.2 Water resources — 34
5.3 Energy resources — 35
5.4 Electricity — 36
5.5 Case study: The Rheidol HEP scheme — 38

6 Population — 40

6.1 Families — 40
6.2 The population census — 41
6.3 Population density — 43
6.4 The quality of our lives — 44

7 Settlement — 45

7.1 Settlement types — 45
7.2 Studying villages — 47
7.3 Studying housing — 52
7.4 Shopping — 54
7.5 Land uses in town — 58
7.6 The quality of our local environment — 60

8 Transport — 62

8.1 Journey to school — 62
8.2 Measuring traffic flow — 63
8.3 Car parking — 65
8.4 Choosing a by-pass route — 67
8.5 Networks and accessibility — 68
8.6 Map study of Chester — 70
8.7 Major transport routes in Britain — 70

9 Farming — 73

9.1 Food and farming — 73
9.2 The farming system — 74
9.3 Farm case studies — 75
     The Hereford farm game — 80

10 Industry — 83

10.1 What is industry? — 83
10.2 The location of industry — 84
10.3 Salt in Cheshire: a Primary industry — 86
10.4 The Nissan car factory in North East
      England: a Secondary industry — 89
10.5 Chester Business Park — 90

11 Recreation — 92

11.1 Local patterns of recreation — 92
11.2 Holidays — 94
11.3 National Parks — 96
11.4 Case Study: Recreation in
      Dartmoor National Park — 98

12 The natural environment — 100

12.1 What is an ecosystem? — 100
12.2 Studying wildlife in the local
      environment — 101
12.3 Wildlife in derelict areas — 103
12.4 Pollution in a small stream — 105

Map extracts — 108

Symbols — 110

Mental maps sometimes turn out to be quite inaccurate when we go out and check them. This shows how important fieldwork and careful observation are if a map is to be accurate.

Figure 2 shows the local area where Frances lives. This is her **local environment**. It is also a sketch map. Figure 3 is the local environment around Frances' school.

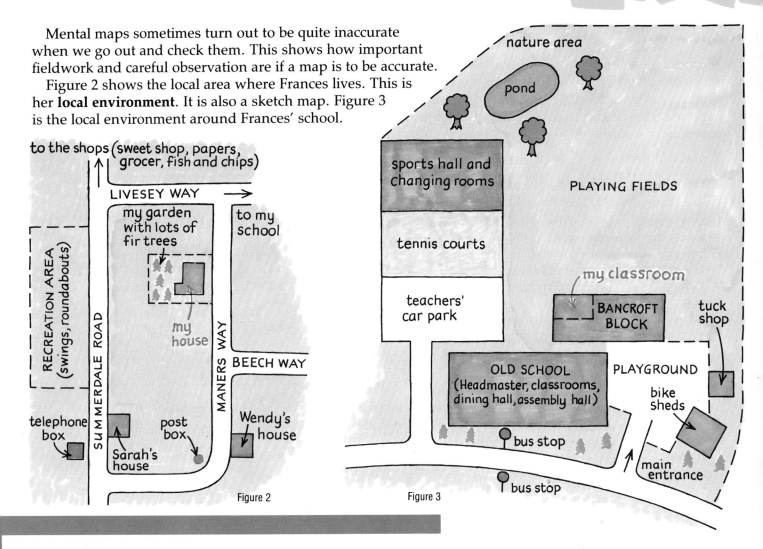

Figure 2

Figure 3

Activities

1 a Either – Draw a simple mental map of your journey to school showing as many important landmarks as you can;
   or – Draw a simple mental map of your local home environment. Again, show as many landmarks as you can remember.

  b At the next opportunity, try out your map to see how accurate it is. Now re-draw the map making it as accurate as possible.

  c Write a few sentences describing what you have learnt from this activity. How well did you really know your route to school or local home environment?

2 Produce a sketch map of your school environment rather like that in Figure 3. To do this, you should walk around the school environment preparing a rough sketch map. Try to show as much detail as possible and don't forget to include important landmarks. You could work in pairs to collect the information. Back in the classroom, produce a neat version of your map and give it the title; '*My local school environment*'.

3 Your parents have agreed for you to hold a party at home. Once you have got over the shock (!) you decide to include a sketch map of how to get to your house on the invitations. Your sketch should show the way to your home from the major roads along which your friends are likely to travel. Produce a clear and accurate map using colours if you wish. Use arrows to show the route.

1.3 Understanding Maps

Most of you will be familiar with the **Ordnance Survey (OS)** maps of Britain. These detailed maps are of great value when plotting routes or locating ourselves to see what is nearby.

Before reading and understanding the Ordnance Survey maps, it is important to know a few basic points.

Scales and distances

All accurate maps should have a **scale**. The scale tells us how distance on a map relates to distance on the ground. There are several ways that scale might be shown (see Figure 1).

Maps can be **large scale** or **small scale**. Figure 2 explains the difference – it is often confusing.

The most widely used OS maps have a scale of 1:50 000. This means that 1 cm on the map is equal to 50 000 cms on the ground. (*2 cms on a 1:50 000 map are equal to 1 kilometre on the ground*). An example of a 1:50 000 map is on page 108.

A more detailed **large** scale OS map is the 1:25 000 map. On this map, 4 cms equal 1 kilometre. See page 109. Compare this with the 1:50 000 extract on page 108 to notice the differences. See how the 1:25 000 extract shows more detail.

The scale is used to measure distance. It is easy to do this if the distance is a **straight line** as the length can be marked onto a piece of paper which can then be placed alongside the linear scale on the map. It is rather more time consuming to measure a **curved** distance (see Figure 3).

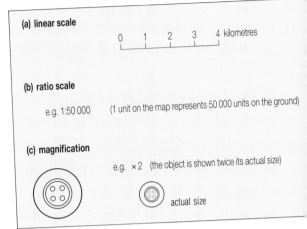

(a) linear scale

(b) ratio scale

e.g. 1:50 000   (1 unit on the map represents 50 000 units on the ground)

(c) magnification

e.g. × 2   (the object is shown twice its actual size)

actual size

Figure 1

Figure 2

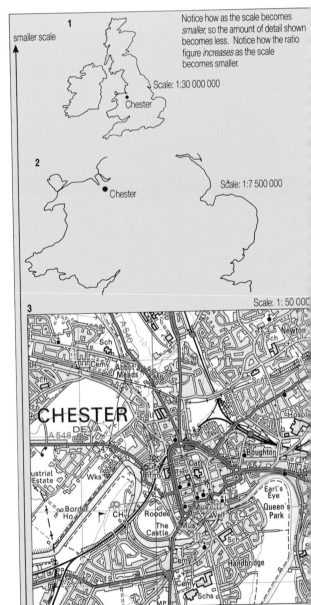

Notice how as the scale becomes *smaller*, so the amount of detail shown becomes less. Notice how the ratio figure *increases* as the scale becomes smaller.

1   smaller scale   Scale: 1:30 000 000   Chester

2   Chester   Scale: 1:7 500 000

3   Scale: 1: 50 000

CHESTER

Figure 3

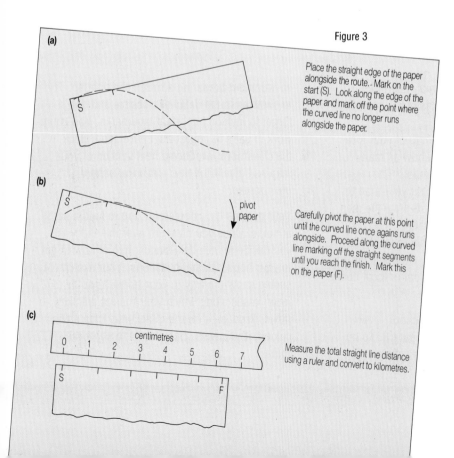

(a) Place the straight edge of the paper alongside the route. Mark on the start (S). Look along the edge of the paper and mark off the point where the curved line no longer runs alongside the paper.

(b) pivot paper   Carefully pivot the paper at this point until the curved line once agains runs alongside. Proceed along the curved line marking off the straight segments until you reach the finish. Mark this on the paper (F).

(c) centimetres   Measure the total straight line distance using a ruler and convert to kilometres.

Activities

1 Figure 4 contains three maps (**a – c**) drawn to different scales. Arrange them in order with the *largest* scale map first and the *smallest* scale last.

2 Working in pairs or in small groups produce a scaled map of your classroom. To do this you should first draw a *sketch map* showing the walls and the main items of furniture. Then use a ruler or tape measure to measure the walls and furniture writing the measurements on your rough sketch.

Now produce a neat and accurate map of your classroom. Work out a scale (e.g. 2cms = 1 metre) and carefully draw your map using a sharp pencil and ruler.

When complete, label the furniture and write your scale in the key.

Figure 4

a

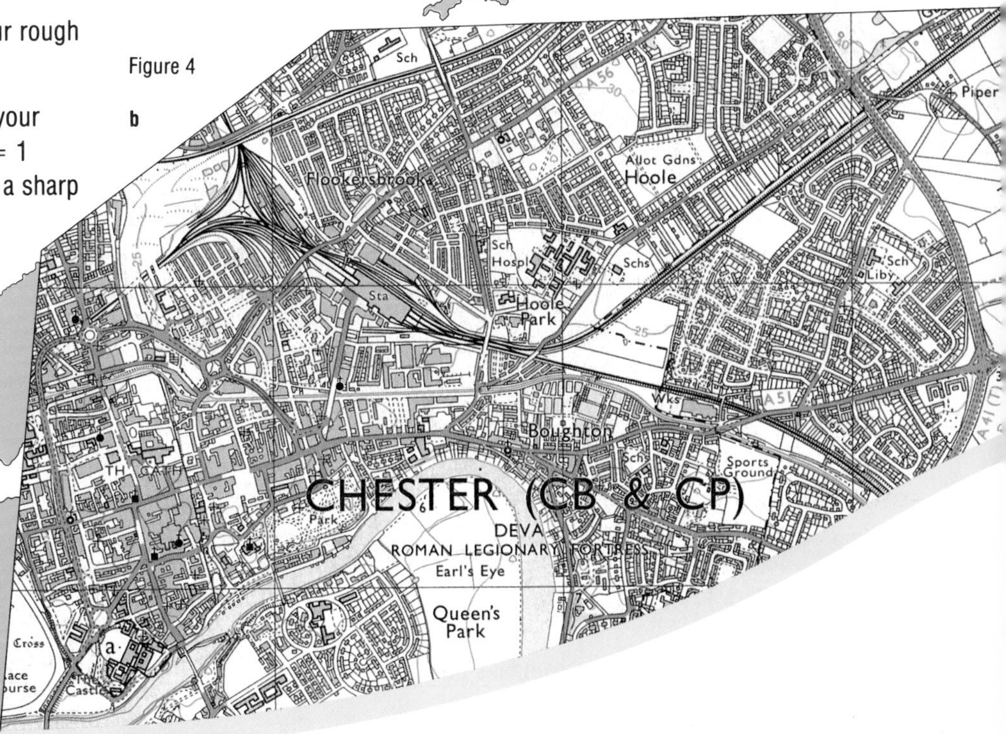

b

c

CHESTER (CB & CP)

3 Study Figure 5. It is a drawing of Ben's room. The room actually measures
4 metres (the window wall) by 3 metres (the bed wall). Ben's bed measures 2 metres by 1 metre. His desk is 2 metres long by 0.75 metre wide. Attempt to draw an accurate map (plan) of Ben's room. Remember that a map looks straight down, so you do not need to worry about the pictures on the wall. You will need to estimate measurements for some of his furniture, although you could measure similar items in your own home to help you.
Don't forget to give your map a title and to explain any symbols used in a key.

Figure 5

Directions

It is important to know about directions particularly when following a route. Directions can be expressed as **compass points** or **bearings**. You may have come across these, possibly in Maths.

On most maps, north is 'straight up'. *But – beware!* Look carefully to check!

Figure 6 shows the 16 points of the compass and the bearings. Figure 7 explains how to take readings of bearings.

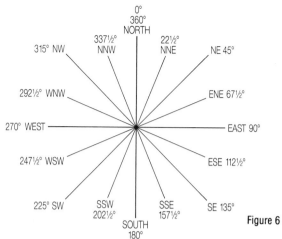

Figure 6

Note that "grid" north on maps is not quite "true" north. This is because it is impossible to show a spherical earth on a flat map.

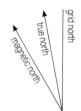

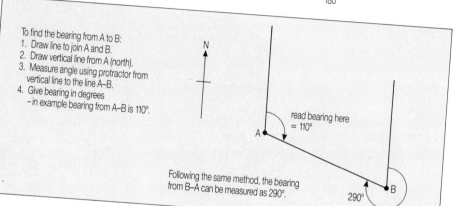

To find the bearing from A to B:
1. Draw line to join A and B.
2. Draw vertical line from A (north).
3. Measure angle using protractor from vertical line to the line A–B.
4. Give bearing in degrees
   – in example bearing from A–B is 110°.

read bearing here = 110°

Following the same method, the bearing from B–A can be measured as 290°.

Figure 7

Activities

4 Give **bearings** for the following **compass points**:
   a south
   b south west
   c north north west
   d east
   e west south west

5 You are the chief navigator of the pirate ship 'Nikker'. Having just robbed and sunk the Games Carrier 'Timelord', your ship is due to take the cargo of computer games into a small inlet to smuggle the games ashore at *Jedi Beach* (see Figure 8). The inlet is narrow and there are many dangers. Your job is to work out a safe route to Jedi Beach. Make a tracing of Figure 8 and plot your route as a series of straight lines. Give each line a number and make a list of the bearings and distances of each line – these are the readings that you would need to give the Captain.

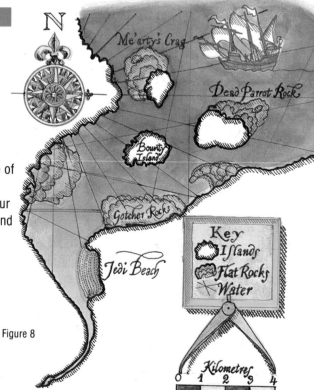

Figure 8

Symbols

The Ordnance Survey uses a standard set of symbols for its maps. Those for the 1:50 000 maps and for the 1:25 000 maps are shown on pages 108 and 109. It is very important that you try to learn as many of these as possible so that you can read maps quickly and accurately.

Activities

6 Figure 9 is a sketch map of a village drawn by a girl on a fieldtrip. Use the 1:50 000 OS symbols at the back of the book to redraw the field sketch. (You could do a similar Activity for your own local area.)

7 Father Christmas was delivering presents one Christmas when he came across a small island. As he flew over the island in search of sherry for himself and hay for Rudolf (or, was it sherry for Rudolf and hay for himself?) he described what he saw – see Figure 10.

On his return to Lapland he wants you, as his chief elf mapmaker, to produce a map of the island. You should be as accurate as possible and should use OS 1:50 000 map symbols where possible. These and any other symbols should be explained in a key. You can make up a name for the island.

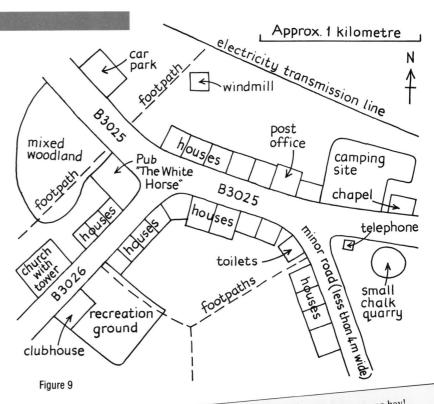

Figure 9

Figure 10

Santa circled the island at high altitude. He noticed that it was roughly pear-shaped and that it was orientated in a north-south direction with the widest part (30kms) in the south. Santa estimated the island to be about 45 kms in length.

In the centre of the island Santa spotted a high mountain and he had to climb to 1500 metres in order to pass safely over it. Looking straight down at the mountain Santa saw that there was a crater on the summit – it was a volcano! Several rivers rushed down the slopes through forests to the sea the largest of which flowed in a series of wide curves in a north-westerly direction.

Santa decided to follow the course of this major river. About a third of the way from the volcano to the coast he came across a small town. Sherry he thought! He descended to take a closer look. The town was roughly circular in shape. There were landing stages along the river and a small number of boats moored alongside. In the centre of the town Santa spotted a market, a church and a foot-

ball field – these islanders must be civilised, he thought. The rest of the town was housing – mostly simple mud huts. He could only see a single road leading out of the town heading due north-east for about 5 kms to a small bauxite mining settlement. A single mineral line ran alongside the road – the bauxite would be taken from the mine along this line, Santa thought. Around the town Santa could see fields of sugar cane, wheat and vegetables. Close to the river there seemed to be a few fields of rice.

Sadly, Santa saw no mince pies and there was no hay for Rudolf who sighed. So, off they went again following the river. As it neared the coast, Santa could see more housing. This must be a port, he thought. Indeed, the town was about twice the size of the inland town extending for about 5 kms along the coast and about 3 kms inland along the river. At the mouth of the river was a harbour with several quays and ships.

Santa sniffed the aroma of mince pies and descended into the town. Luckily he found a

plentiful supply on a ship. However, no hay! Poor Rudolf!

Santa lifted off and circled high above the port to see if he could spot some hay. The northern tip of the island appeared to be all forest. The northern coast seemed to be rocky with steep cliffs. No hay!

He decided to head south along the west coast of the island. Much of the coast was low lying with lagoons and sand dunes. It looked lovely for a swim but Rudolf was not in the mood. To his left he saw the volcano again looming up in the distance some 15 kms away.

By now Santa was sure that most of the island was forested. However, from the volcano to the south coast the vegetation was different – it was a huge coffee plantation. On the south coast Santa saw another port about the same size as the other port. Several small roads radiated inland from the port into the coffee plantation.

Just to the east of the town there were fields of food crops and, could it really be?......yes, it looked like it...HAY! 'Yippee', said Rudolf.

1.4   Using maps

Grid References

Most maps contain grids which are used to pinpoint the location of, for example, a town. You will probably already have used grids and co-ordinates in Maths, so this idea will be familiar to you.

In Geography, we use **four – figure grid references** to locate whole grids and **six – figure grid references** to locate points. Figure 1 explains how to take grid references and many of the Activities at the end of this chapter make use of them. It is quite easy, but *be careful*!

Figure 1

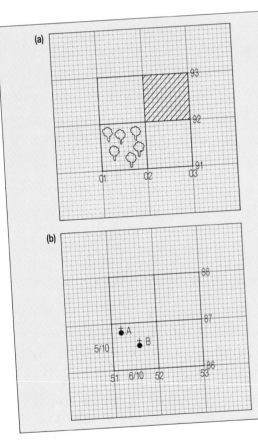

How to find grid references

Look carefully at the map extract on page 108. Notice that the map has been divided into many boxes. These are called grid squares. Each grid line has a number which is written at the edge of the map. Numbers increase in two directions:

1   from left to right across the map (these lines are called eastings);
2   from bottom to top across the map (these lines are called northings).

You must remember two rules when finding a grid reference:

1   the number written against each grid line refers to the next square along;
2   the easting number is always given before the northing number ('along the corridor and up the stairs').

Four-figure reference

Study Figure (a). The shaded square can be given the reference 0292 as it is the square after the easting line reading 02 and the northing line reading 92. The reference is said as 'nought two, nine two'.

Six-figure reference

To find a six-figure reference, we imagine that each square is divided into tenths. This has been done for the square containing the churches (Figure (b)). Church B lies six-tenths of the way between 51 and 52. This is written as 516 and makes up the first three figures of the six-figure reference. Looking along the northing line, church B is five-tenths of the way between 86 and 87. This is written as 865 and makes up the second three figures.

Thus, the complete six-figure reference reads 516865. It is said 'five one, six, eight six five'. While it is possible to divide each grid square with a ruler, it is good enough to make a careful estimate. What is the reference of church A?

Contour patterns

One of the most useful bits of information on a Ordnance Survey map concerns the **relief** or 'lie of the land'. The height above sea level is shown by **triangulation pillars, spot heights** and **contours**. Contours are lines joining up points of equal height above sea level. They are drawn at regular height intervals, e.g. at every 10 metres on a 1:50 000 map.

The patterns of contours can be used to give us an idea of what the landscape looks like. Figure 2 explains some common contour patterns. With plenty of experience it is possible to 'see' a landscape by just looking at a map!

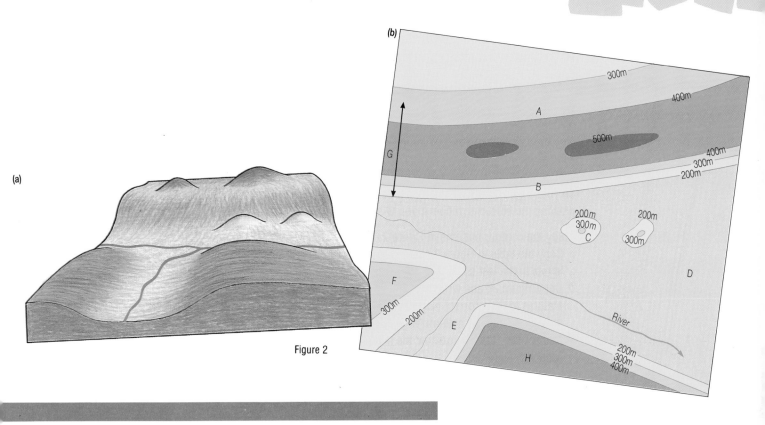

(a)

(b)

Figure 2

Activities

These Activities are based entirely on the map extracts on pages 108–9.

1 Refer to the map extract on page 108.
  a What is found at
   ● 413627   ● 405694
   ● 378703   ● 447688
   ● 365707   ● 420671
  b Give four – figure grid references for the following:
   ● Mollington village
   ● marshes at Huntington (just south of Chester)
   ● centre of Chester
  c Give the six – figure grid references for:
   ● post office in Eccleston
   ● church with tower in Backford
   ● town hall in Chester
   ● level crossing at Balderton
   ● Christleton school
2 Use the map extract on page 108 to follow the route described below carefully completing the blank spaces.
  Otto was a young otter with a keen sense of adventure. One day he set off from his river bank home opposite the milepost in the 'Crook of Dee' in grid square .... in a northerly direction. As

he swam along enjoying the warmth of the sun on his back he noticed people walking along the .... to his left. It wasn't long before he reached Ferry Farm at .... Here he met up with his friend Rocky 4, the water rat.

After exchanging greetings the animals continued on their way and soon passed the village of .... Looking to the east, they were unable to see much because the river bank was lined with .... Soon they passed beneath a bridge carrying the .... The noise frightened them and they ran to Heronbridge. Here they met up with Hetty the heron.

Hetty offered to show her friends something of the countryside. Hetty flew from Heronbridge in a WSW direction passing over a school to then circle over the .... at 393635. Rocky 4, being a bit of a wizz-rat, estimated that it was about .... metres above sea level.

Now flying south, Hetty took her friends over the major road junction at .... She soon flew on as the fumes made her cough and splutter. She turned east to the village of .... and then SSE to Eaton Hall. There was a big lake in grid square .... which the owners of the Hall kept well stocked with trout. Hetty landed close to the lake and her passengers dived into the water to catch their tea.

After tea, Otto and Rocky 4 headed back to the 'Crook of Dee'. By the time Otto got home he was very tired as he had travelled a total of .... kilometres.

You can make up your own story and try it out on your friends. The 'blanks' could be filled in by drawing the correct symbols if you wish.

3 Study the contour patterns in Figure 2.
  a Copy the table in Figure 3 and put the correct letters in the last column.
  b Copy Figure 2b and write the names of the features in their correct places. Use increasingly darker colours (e.g. yellow, orange, red, brown) to show the higher ground.

4 Study the map extract on page 108.
  a Is most of the extract at 0–30 metres; 30–60 metres; 60 metres +?
  b Locate grid squares 3971 and 4171. In which square are the steepest slopes?
  c Locate grid square 3969. Draw a simple sketch

Feature	Description	Letter
HILL	An isolated area of high ground	
SPUR	A finger of high ground	
GENTLE SLOPE	A gentle slope!	
PLAIN	A flat lowland area usually quite large	
PLATEAU	A flat-topped area of high ground often with steep sides	
STEEP SLOPE	A steep slope!	
VALLEY	A dip in the landscape between uplands often containing a river in the bottom	
ESCARPMENT	An upland ridge with one steep slope (SCARP) and one gentle slope (DIP SLOPE)	

Figure 3

of this grid square and mark on the contours and the river. Clearly label the following features: – *valley; steep slope; gentle slope; canal.* Write on the grid numbers too.

  d Turn to the map extract on page 109 (1:25 000). Make a tracing of the contours in the grid square 4164. Label as many relief features as you can. Don't forget to write the height alongside each contour.

1.5   Using an atlas

Modern school atlases contain a great deal of useful information for the geographer. Apart from ordinary maps, they give details about climate, physical features, wealth, agriculture, population and so on. Have a careful look through your atlas to see what it contains.

Turn to the **index** at the back of your atlas. The index lists all places, rivers, lakes and mountains that are located somewhere in the atlas. Notice that it is organised in alphabetical order.

Figure 1 describes how to find the city of **Manchester** in the UK. Notice that Manchester is located using lines of **latitude** and **longitude** in much the same way that grid references are used on an Ordnance Survey map.

Figure 1

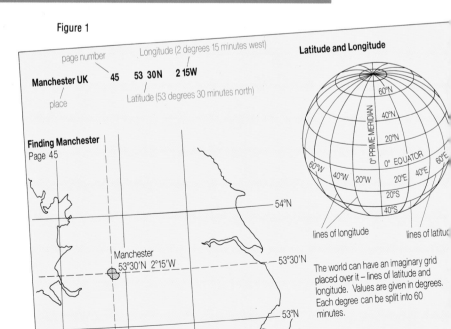

The world can have an imaginary grid placed over it – lines of latitude and longitude. Values are given in degrees. Each degree can be split into 60 minutes.

Activities

1 For this Activity you need a blank outline of the British Isles.

  a Use a ruler to draw the following lines of latitude: 50°N; 52°N; 54°N; 56°N; 58°N. Now mark on the following lines of longitude: 0; 2°W; 4°W; 6°W; 8°W. Label each line clearly.

  b Look up the following in the index of your atlas and locate them on your map
  - Belfast
  - Southampton
  - Rotherham
  - Snowdon (Mt.)
  - Windermere (Lake)
  - Hereford
  - Bodmin Moor
  - Loch Lomond
  - Nuneaton
  - Lough Neagh

  c Make up a list of 10 **lakes** for a friend to locate using the index.

Dictionary

bearings angles taken from the vertical which show direction.

contours lines joining points of equal height above sea level.

grid references the method of pinpointing areas or points on a map using the grid numbers.

latitude imaginary lines drawn parallel with the equator around the world.

longitude imaginary lines drawn parallel with the **prime meridian** – a line joining North and South Poles and running through Greenwich in London.

mental map a map of an area drawn from memory. It will not always be completely accurate.

relief the ups and downs of the landscape; the 'lie' of the land. (See Figure 3, Section 1.4 for definitions of some relief features)

scale the way of showing by how much a map differs from the real world. *Large* scale maps show greater detail than *small* scale maps.

triangulation pillar a white pillar placed on a high point overlooking the landscape and used for surveying. The height in metres is given alongside the symbol on a map.

2 Sense of place

2.1   A Sense of Place in Britain

How many of you could place your home town or village on a map of Britain? It might be fun to have a go and compare your position with others in the class.

Your positioning reflects your **perception** of where your town or village is in relation to other places. Perception is the way we, as individuals, see things. Each one of us has a slightly different perception from our friends. You will come across this word in later chapters as it often helps to explain why people do things.

It is important to know some basic information about the **geography** of Britain – where the main towns are, for example.

First of all, what do we mean by **Great Britain** and how does it differ from the **United Kingdom** and the **British Isles**? Figure 1 explains the differences – take time to learn which is which and try to use each term correctly.

The following activities are intended to help you learn some basic details about the geography of the British Isles.

Great Britain

United Kingdom

Figure 1

British Isles

Activities

1 Study Figure 2. It shows some of the seas/channels and islands off the mainland of Britain. Some have been wrongly labelled. Working on your own or in pairs try to sort out the correct labels for the seas/channels (1–5) and islands (A–G).

Figure 2

2 For this activity your class needs to be divided into teams of three or four as this activity will be run as a quiz. Each team will need an outline map of the UK.

   Figure 3 is a map showing the counties of the UK. Each one has a number. Your teacher will give each team in turn a number. The team should try to name the county to gain 2 points. A question passed over is worth 1 point but an incorrect answer means 1 point deducted.

3 It would be interesting to compare the perceptions of different year groups within your school or to ask your parents. You could see whether accuracy improves with age.

4 It is now important to produce your own map showing the basic geography of the British Isles. To do this you will need an atlas and the answers to the activities above.

   Working in pencil to start with, locate on an outline map of the British Isles:
   ● your home town
   ● your home county and region (see Figure 3)
   ● the seas/channels (Activity 1)
   ● the islands off the mainland (Activity 1)
   ● the borders of England, Wales, Scotland, Northern Ireland and Eire.
   ● major towns and cities

   Now use colours and ink labels to complete your map.

Figure 3

Dictionary

Britain England, Wales, Scotland

United Kingdom England, Wales, Scotland, N. Ireland

British Isles England, Wales, Scotland, Ireland

3 Physical Geography

3.1 The physical geography of Britain

Physical geography is the study of landscapes and the processes which form them.

We are very lucky in Britain to have a great variety of landscapes – some are shown on Figure 1. There are rugged mountains in the Lake District and Scotland (Figure 1a), rolling hilly landscapes in Yorkshire (Figure 1b), and huge flat farmlands in Lincolnshire and East Anglia (Figure 1d). We don't have to travel for very long before we pass into very different scenery from that in which we live.

Have you ever thought how some of these landscapes have been formed?

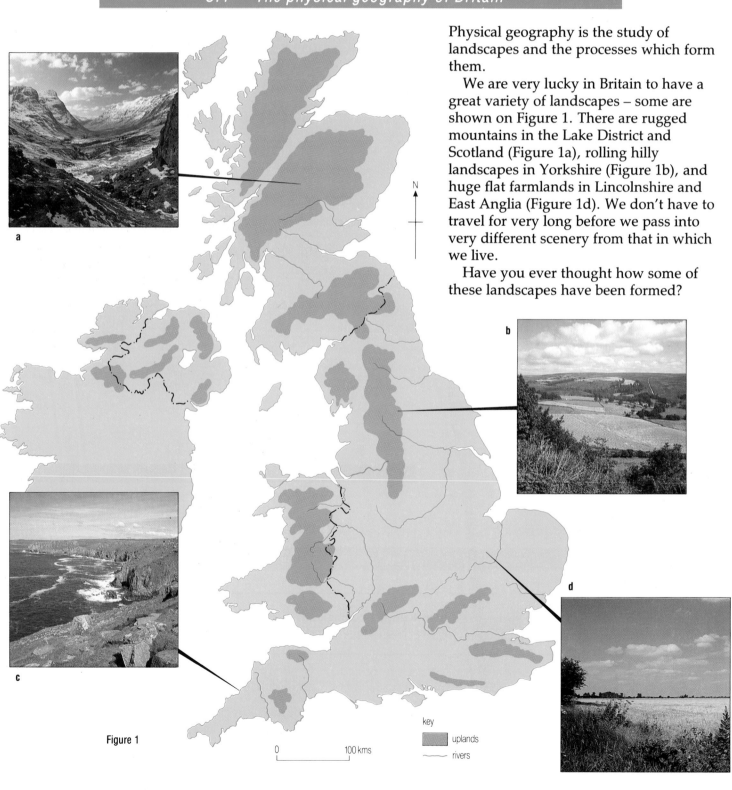

Figure 1

key
- uplands
- rivers

0   100 kms

In Britain, one of the main sculptors of the landscape is water (**rivers**) (see page 18). In picking up and removing particles of rock and soil they **erode** the landscape. Rivers are not the only form of erosion – the sea, wind and ice are other **agents of erosion**.

Although we can see the effect of rivers and the sea today, one important process which had a great effect on our landscape in the past is ice. (You will learn more about the work of ice in *Exploring Geography* 2.)

Activities

1 Write a description of a landscape which you have visited recently, perhaps during your last holiday. Draw a map to show its location and, if possible, use photographs, postcards or drawings to illustrate your account. Describe what the landscape is like (steep? rugged? gentle hills?). Refer to the colours of the landscape. What did you do whilst you were there? What are the main uses of the landscape (farming? mining? tourism?)?

2 Which of the landscapes in Figure 1 do you like the most? Why?

3 As a class, construct a wall display to show the different landscapes in Britain. To do this you could use postcards, newspaper photographs or travel brochures from travel agents. You could try to display them alongside a map of Britain to show where they are located.

4 For this Activity you will need a large outline map of Britain. You will also need to turn to an atlas map showing the **physical geography** of Britain. From Figure 1, make a copy of the uplands and the rivers in pencil first. Then use blue lines to show the rivers and brown shading to show the uplands. Use your atlas to name the uplands and the rivers either straight onto the map or in a key. Finally, plot the location of your home town.

3.2   Weathering

Look at Figure 1. It shows a gargoyle on Saint Paul's Cathedral. It has lost most of the fine detail of its features. This is the result of **weathering**. If you look around you on your journey from home to school you may see other signs of weathering e.g. buildings discoloured or the writing on gravestones no longer being visible.

Weathering is the slow rotting or break down of rocks. Unlike erosion, the rocks and surfaces are not picked up and removed – they stay in the same place.

Figure 1

It is possible to divide weathering into three types:

1 **Physical** – This includes the effect of rapid heating and cooling which is common in desert areas and causes rocks to expand and contract. Soon they begin to break apart.

In mountain areas and cold climates **freeze-thaw** operates. Water in a crack freezes and, on becoming ice, expands (this is why pipes sometimes freeze and then burst in the winter). As it expands it causes the crack to get larger. Then the ice thaws; water fills the enlarged crack; it freezes again, and so the process or **cycle** goes on. Eventually rock fragments will break off. Piles of angular **scree** at the base of mountains are the results of this process.

2 **Chemical** – Rainwater is slightly acidic and it can slowly dissolve rock surfaces, such as in Figure 1. (See page 31 to read about **acid rain**).

3 **Biological** – Tree roots and animal burrows can damage rocks, pavements and buildings. Some of you may have noticed how paving stones are often uneven if there are trees close by.

Weathering and erosion combine to wear away the landscape – this is called **denudation** and results in an overall lowering of the land.

Activities

1 What is the difference between **erosion**, **weathering** and **denudation**?

2 Make a copy of Figure 2 which describes the process of freeze-thaw. Add labels or write a few sentences to describe how the process operates.

3 Carry out a survey of weathering in your school grounds.

To do this you will need a plan of the school grounds, a clipboard and pencil and a copy of the record sheet in Figure 3. Before you do your survey, study Figure 4 to remind you of some of the effects of weathering which you can look out for.

Walk around the school grounds looking for signs of weathering. Concentrate on the buildings and look particularly at ledges.

Do not work on old or crumbling walls.

Mark each location on your map and give it a reference number. Then complete the record sheet. Take time over drawing sketches and remember to include a scale and labels.

When you get back into the classroom make a neat and careful copy of your results. You could do this as a table or as a series of box labels alongside a map of your school grounds.

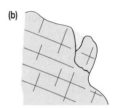 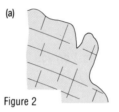 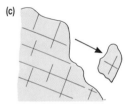

Figure 2

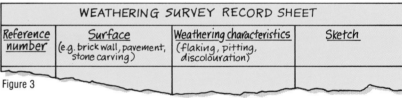

Reference number	Surface (e.g. brick wall, pavement, stone carving)	Weathering characteristics (flaking, pitting, discolouration)	Sketch

WEATHERING SURVEY RECORD SHEET

Figure 3

Figure 4 Effects of weathering

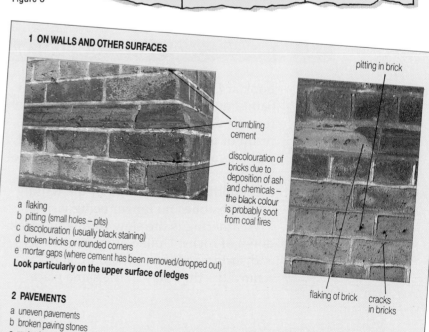

1 ON WALLS AND OTHER SURFACES

a flaking
b pitting (small holes – pits)
c discolouration (usually black staining)
d broken bricks or rounded corners
e mortar gaps (where cement has been removed/dropped out)
Look particularly on the upper surface of ledges

2 PAVEMENTS

a uneven pavements
b broken paving stones
c roots showing on surface

crumbling cement

discolouration of bricks due to deposition of ash and chemicals – the black colour is probably soot from coal fires

pitting in brick

flaking of brick   cracks in bricks

a Is there any relationship between the way a wall faces and the extent of weathering? We might expect there to be more severe weathering on a south-west facing wall as this is the most common (**prevailing**) wind direction. Is this the case with your school?

b Is there any relationship between the amount of weathering and the age of a wall? Try to find out the ages of your school walls – your caretaker or maintenance department might know.

3.3   Slopes

There are not many areas where the ground is completely flat. Most areas are on a **slope**. It is possible to identify several different types of slope.

Measuring slopes is a very important part of **surveying**. For example, if a new road, railway or airport runway is to be built, the slope of the ground must be known. Although experienced surveyors use expensive and complex equipment we can measure slopes fairly accurately using simple instruments.

Activities

1 An instrument that can be used to measure slopes is a **clinometer**. The instructions for making a simple clinometer are given in Figure 1. Have a go at making your own.

Figure 1

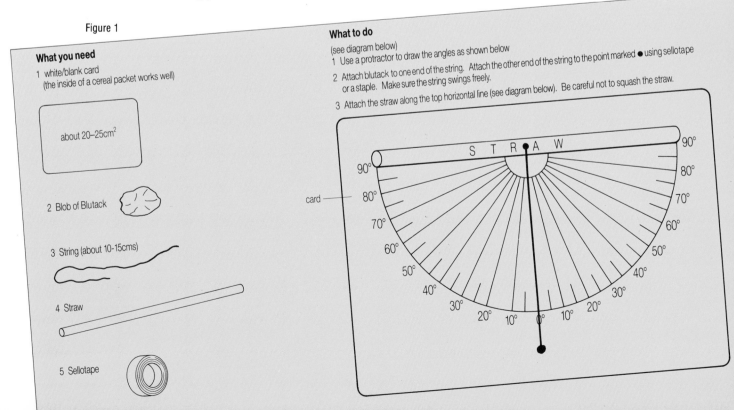

What you need
1 white/blank card
   (the inside of a cereal packet works well)

   about 20–25cm²

2 Blob of Blutack

3 String (about 10-15cms)

4 Straw

5 Sellotape

What to do
(see diagram below)
1 Use a protractor to draw the angles as shown below
2 Attach blutack to one end of the string. Attach the other end of the string to the point marked ● using sellotape or a staple. Make sure the string swings freely.
3 Attach the straw along the top horizontal line (see diagram below). Be careful not to squash the straw.

card —

2 Look carefully at Figure 2. It describes how a group of pupils carried out a **slope transect** in their school grounds and used it to produce a **slope profile**. Carry out a similar study in your school grounds or in a park close to your school.

3 Figure 3 gives slope and distance readings for a river valley. Using a scale of 1 cm = 10 metres, carefully construct a slope profile of the valley. Label the steepest slope and the river. This is best done by laying a sheet of plain paper or tracing paper over a sheet of graph paper.

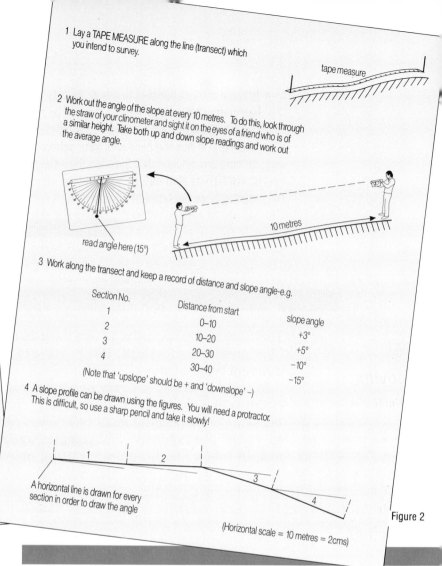

1 Lay a TAPE MEASURE along the line (transect) which you intend to survey.

tape measure

2 Work out the angle of the slope at every 10 metres. To do this, look through the straw of your clinometer and sight it on the eyes of a friend who is of a similar height. Take both up and down slope readings and work out the average angle.

read angle here (15°)

10 metres

3 Work along the transect and keep a record of distance and slope angle—e.g.

Section No.	Distance from start	slope angle
1	0–10	
2	10–20	+3°
3	20–30	+5°
4	30–40	–10°
		–15°

(Note that 'upslope' should be + and 'downslope' –)

4 A slope profile can be drawn using the figures. You will need a protractor. This is difficult, so use a sharp pencil and take it slowly!

A horizontal line is drawn for every section in order to draw the angle

1   2   3   4

(Horizontal scale = 10 metres = 2cms)

Figure 2

Figure 3

Section number	Distance from start (metres)	Slope angle (degrees)
1	0–10	–10
2	10–20	–15
3	20–30	–25
4	30–40	–30
5	40–50	–20
6	50–60	–5
7	60–70	0
8	70–80	+10
9	80–90	+35
10	90–100	+20
11	100–110	+10
12	110–120	+5

(River is between 63 and 64 metres from start)

− decrease (downslope)
+ increase (upslope)

3.4   Rivers

We have already seen in Chapter 3.1 how rivers are very important in shaping our landscape. Rivers transfer water and **sediment** (particles of rock and soil) from uplands to the sea and as they do so they shape our landscape by eroding and depositing.

Look at the two photographs Figures 1 and 2. Figure 1 shows part of the River Dart in Devon. Notice that it is a quite wide but shallow river. The water is clear suggesting that not much sediment is being carried. The river bed is made of small pebbles. There are some much bigger boulders in the photograph which have been used to make stepping stones across the river.

Figure 1

Figure 2 shows a curve or **meander** in the River Sid also in Devon. Here the river is more murky suggesting that it is carrying quite a lot of sediment. Notice the 'white water'. This is the result of the water flowing over larger stones – it is **turbulence**. As the water swings round the bend, the faster current shifts to the outside of the bend where it erodes and undercuts the bank to form a **river cliff**. The slower current on the inside bend is unable to carry all its sediment so it dumps it to form a **slip-off slope**.

Figure 2

Figure 3

Activities

1 Figure 3 is a sketch of the river in Figure 2. Make a copy of the sketch and add labels to show the following:
- direction of river flow
- path of the fastest current
- erosion of the outside bank
- deposition on the inside bend
- river cliff
- slip-off slope
- turbulence

2 The best way to understand more about rivers is to study a short section of a small river or stream. There is probably one close to your school. There are several aspects that can easily be studied:

a Make a simple sketch map of the section of river. Mark on any features such as boulders, turbulence, river cliffs, slip-off slopes and meanders. Float small twigs down the river to work out the course of the fastest current – do this several times as boulders, overhanging branches or the wind might give a false result. Use a tape measure to work out an approximate scale.

b Discover the depth and width of a section across the river (see Figure 4). Figure 5 describes how to obtain the readings and gives you a sample record sheet. You can then use your results to produce a **cross section** across the river (Figure 6). Interesting features can be labelled.

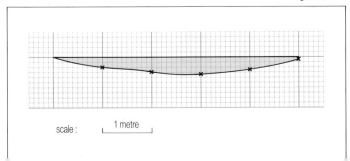

Figure 4

Figure 6

scale :   1 metre

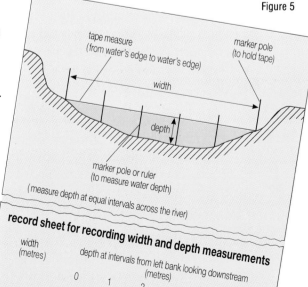

Figure 5

tape measure (from water's edge to water's edge)

marker pole (to hold tape)

width

depth

marker pole or ruler (to measure water depth)

(measure depth at equal intervals across the river)

record sheet for recording width and depth measurements

width (metres)	depth at intervals from left bank looking downstream (metres)					
	0	1	2	3	4	5
5	0	0.2	0.3	0.35	0.25	0.04

c Discover the amount of water passing through a section of the river. This is called the river's **discharge**. To find this you need to discover two things:

1 the **area** of the cross section
2 the speed of water called the **velocity**

To discover the area, you need to count the squares in your cross section drawn in b above and work out the area in **square metres**.
To discover the velocity, you need to follow the instructions given in Figure 7.

Now, carry out the following:

area (square metres) x **velocity** (metres per second)
= **discharge** (cubic metres per second)

Your final figure will probably be surprisingly small!

d Discover what sort of material is being carried by the river. You could place an empty milk bottle in the river facing upstream to collect a water sample. Let it settle or pass it through filter paper to discover what material is being carried within the river.

You could study the stones on the river bed. Take 30 pebbles at random and use a ruler to measure the long axis (see Figure 8). Add up all your results and divide by 30 to find the **average size**. Discover the **roundness** of your 30 pebbles by giving each one a value (see Figure 9). Again, work out the average by adding together all your numbers and dividing by 30.

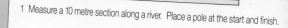

1 Measure a 10 metre section along a river. Place a pole at the start and finish.

2 Time a float (an orange is ideal) over the 10 metre distance.

3 Repeat this 3 or 5 times releasing the float at different points across the river.

4 Find an average time taken (in seconds) to cover the 10 metre section.

5 To find velocity –

$$\frac{10 \text{ (the distance in metres)}}{\text{average time (seconds)}} = \text{VELOCITY (metres per second)}$$

Figure 7 Finding velocity

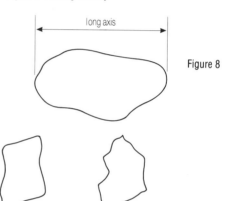

long axis

Figure 8

well-rounded (value=1)   rounded (value=2)   sub-rounded (value=3)   sub-angular (value=4)   angular (value=5)   very angular (value=6)   Figure 9

3 A group of pupils carried out a survey of their local river at two different points 10 kilometres apart. Their results are given in Figure 10.
   a Use these results to plot cross sections and then discover the **discharge** for both points.
   b Try to suggest reasons for any difference in discharge.

Velocity Readings	
Location	Time taken to travel 10 metres (5 readings taken)
1	18, 19, 24, 22, 17
2	20, 26, 31, 23, 25
(Use these figures to find the average time taken and then divide the distance (10) by the average time to find the velocity in metres per second)	

	Width (metres)	Depth (metres) Distance (metres) from left bank								
		0	1	2	3	4	5	6	7	8
1 (upstream)	4	0	0.3	0.4	0.2	0.2	–	–	–	–
2 (downstream)	8	0.2	0.3	0.5	0.5	0.2	0.4	0.1	0.1	0

(Use these figures to plot cross sections – use the same scale as on Figure 6. Find the area by counting the squares – 100 small squares = 1 m²)

Figure 10

Drainage Basins

A river and the streams that join it (called **tributaries**) drain an area of land called a **drainage basin** (see Figure 11). A drainage basin is named after the main river that drains it, for example, the River Tees drainage basin.

There are a number of important terms on Figure 11 which you should take time to learn. Look in the Dictionary at the end of this chapter to discover their meaning.

When rain falls onto a drainage basin it tends to soak into the soil and then slowly passes through soil and rock until it reaches the river channel (see Figure 12). Water on the ground surface may **evaporate** into the air. It then rises and cools. This leads to **condensation** and the formation of clouds. Rain may then occur. This is the **water cycle** (see page 29).

Figure 11

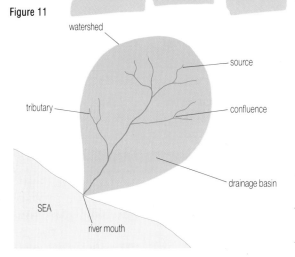

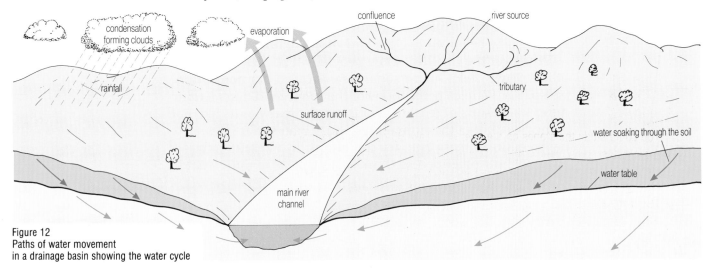

Figure 12
Paths of water movement
in a drainage basin showing the water cycle

Activities

1 a Look back to Figure 12 which shows the way in which water reaches a river. How do you think the following drainage basin characteristics would affect the speed of water movement? Give reasons for your answers.
  ● steep slopes ● sandy soils ● large areas covered by tarmac ● dense network of drains running beneath the surface ● heavily forested or grassed drainage basin
 b Now make a list of as many drainage basin characteristics as you can that would lead to rapid water movement in a river and possible flooding. You could use a diagram to show the factors.

Dictionary

confluence the point where two tributaries meet.
denudation the lowering of the land by erosion and weathering.
discharge the amount of water passing along a river channel.
erosion removal of particles of rock or soil by agents of erosion.
sediment rock fragments transported by water, wind.
slip-off slope sediment usually deposited on the inside of a meander.
surface runoff water flowing over the ground when it is unable to soak into the soil.
tributary a small stream that joins a larger stream or river.
watershed the edge of the drainage basin.
water table the upper surface of underground water.

4 Weather

Many of you probably look forward to snow in winter. Snowball fights, sledging, ice slides in the playground and possibly even the cancellation of school!

However, not everyone likes the snow. Drivers face dangerous conditions on the roads, the elderly suffer from the cold, farm animals may be stranded on hills without food, airports may be forced to close and sports fixtures abandoned.

Whatever the weather, some people will be pleased and others displeased. Our personal view is called our **perception** (see p. 12). Peoples perceptions of the same conditions tend to differ for all sorts of reasons. For example, many of us like hot sunny weather in the summer but those who suffer from hayfever dread these hot, dry conditions. It is helpful to be aware of how other people think as it helps us to understand their behaviour.

Activities

1 Look at the photograph, cartoon and newspaper articles in Figure 1. They describe some of the effects of severe winter conditions.
   a Make a list of the different people affected by the winter weather. For each person, describe *how* the weather has affected them.
   b Are most of the people pleased or displeased with the weather conditions?

Figure 1

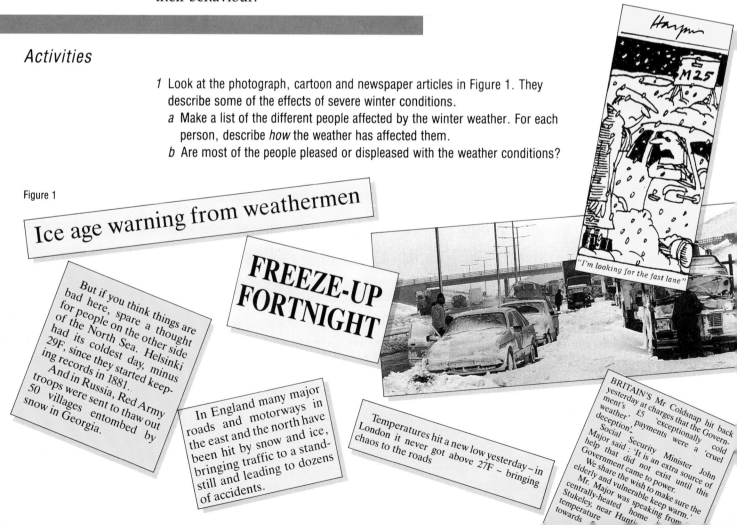

Ice age warning from weathermen

FREEZE-UP FORTNIGHT

But if you think things are bad here, spare a thought for people on the other side of the North Sea. Helsinki had its coldest day, minus 29F, since they started keeping records in 1881.
And in Russia, Red Army troops were sent to thaw out 50 villages entombed by snow in Georgia.

In England many major roads and motorways in the east and the north have been hit by snow and ice, bringing traffic to a standstill and leading to dozens of accidents.

Temperatures hit a new low yesterday – in London it never got above 27F – bringing chaos to the roads

BRITAIN'S Mr Coldsnap hit back yesterday at charges that the Government's £5 'exceptionally cold weather' payments were a 'cruel deception'.
Social Security Minister John Major said : 'It is an extra source of help that did not exist until this Government came to power.
We share the wish to make sure the elderly and vulnerable keep warm.'
Mr. Major was speaking from centrally-heated home in Stukeley, near Hunti temperature towards

"I'm looking for the fast lane"

2 Figure 2 is a cartoon that appeared in a newspaper during a spell of severe winter weather. In pairs, make up a short caption to go with the cartoon. Remember that it should be amusing!

Figure 2

3 June 1989 was a very warm and dry month. Indeed, the Spring of 1989 had also been dry. Figure 3 describes the conditions in June.

a What is your view (your **perception**) of the type of weather described in Figure 3? Now discuss your view with a partner or with a small group. Is your point of view shared by others? Remember that everybody's view is valid – there is no 'right' or 'wrong' answer!

b In small groups discuss the likely views of the following people to the weather described in Figure 3. Give reasons for the views you describe.
 ● a farmer growing salad crops
 ● a long distance lorry or coach driver
 ● a tennis player
 ● a fireman
 ● a builder
 ● a Water Authority official
 ● a pub owner

HIGH AND DRY

Killer drought is worse than 1976

by JULIAN ROLLINS

WATER chiefs were in the dock yesterday as sizzling Britain headed for a drought.

With temperatures hitting 88F°, the hottest June since 1986, supplies are running low and many areas face rationing.

One town has run out of water completely. Householders in Nelson in Lancashire will have to wait until more is diverted to their area.

WEATHERMEN fear Britain is in the grip of the worst drought since 1976.

That cost farmers £500 million in lost production, hit industry and brought huge forest fires.

A Southern Water official said the latest drought would be even worse if the dry weather continued.

The heatwave, which has already led to the deaths of many swimmers trying to cool off, brought more tragedy yesterday. Police warnings failed to stop youngsters diving into chilling inshore waters.

John Gort, 15, from Ashton-Under-Lyne, was only yards away from the bank of a reservoir in Debdale Park, Greater Manchester, when he got into difficulties and disappeared.

And at a mill pond in Greater Manchester, 14-year-old Dale Wray drowned after getting cramp.

Police Inspector Lachlan Carver urged parents to warn children of the dangers of inland water.

"Youngsters simply don't realise how cold the water in these ponds and reservoirs can be," he said.

"When you dive in the shock simply takes your breath away. Cramp can set in very quickly."

Today 21.6.89

Figure 3

4.2   _Forecasting the weather_

Many of you will recognise the face of John Kettley in Figure 1. He is one of several weathermen and women seen on the television. John works at the London Weather Centre producing forecasts for the BBC. He is an expert on the weather.

Figure 1 describes how he produces a typical weather forecast for the BBC.

Notice that the final **weather chart** uses **symbols** to represent different types of weather. The symbols used are clear and easy to understand.

A day in the life of John Kettley

This shows you what I can see from my desk. Everything is automatic – there is no cameraman.

This is me sitting at the desk where I present the hourly forecasts. You can see one of my weather maps on the TV monitor.

This is a satellite picture arriving in the office.

7.00 am: I arrive at the office at the BBC Television Centre. I then study the satellite photos and telex print-outs to find out the state of the weather. I look at reports of the overnight weather too.

7.30 am: I speak to the Meteorological Office (the weather headquarters) at Bracknell to hear their advice about the likely weather for that day.

7.30 – 8.55 am: During this time I prepare the forecasts using a computer to prepare the 20 or so visuals that I might use during a broadcast. It is my own decision as to what I forecast and what I say in my broadcasts.

8.55 am: My first live broadcast of the day! 30 seconds on BBC 1 South East. I follow this with a national broadcast at 9.03am also on BBC 1.

10.00 am/11.00 am: Further broadcasts on BBC 1.

11.30 am: I have another conference with the Met. Office to see if there are any new developments. If there are, I may alter my visuals.

I do another 4 live broadcasts before my shift finishes at 2.00 pm. The major broadcast is at 1.25 pm when I have 2 mins 30 secs.

This is where I present the main broadcasts. It is a small studio and you can see the camera in the foreground. The blue screen is the one you see on the TV forecasts. When the lights are full on, I can hardly see the screen, although I do have a monitor in front of me.

Figure 1

Activities

1 You may need an atlas for this Activity. Look back to the satellite photograph in Figure 3, Unit 4.1.
  a Which parts of the British Isles are cloudless? How can you tell this from the photograph?
  b Which parts of the British Isles have cloud?
  c How useful do you think satellite photographs are in making a weather forecast?

2 In this Activity, you are going to produce a weather chart. Figure 2 contains weather reports from a number of **weather stations** around Britain. Your job is to produce a weather map showing this information.
  a Some of the standard BBC weather symbols are shown in Figure 3 to help you produce a weather chart showing the information in Figure 2. Use an atlas to plot the symbols in their correct locations on an outline map of Britain. Do it in pencil first and then use colours if you wish.
  b Describe in a few sentences the weather in Britain as shown by your chart.

3 In Activity 2 you produced a chart of weather recorded at one moment in time – 6.00 am on 10 July. Now look at Figure 4. This shows the **expected** weather for the same weather stations at 12.00 midday. As this chart looks forward, it is a **forecast**.
  Using your chart completed in Activity 2 and the chart in Figure 4 write a **forecast** for Britain for the morning of 10 July. You may like to work in pairs to do this. Forecasts should be read out to the rest of the class and should take no longer than 1 minute. Watch a weather forecast on the BBC to see how such a forecast is presented.

Figure 3

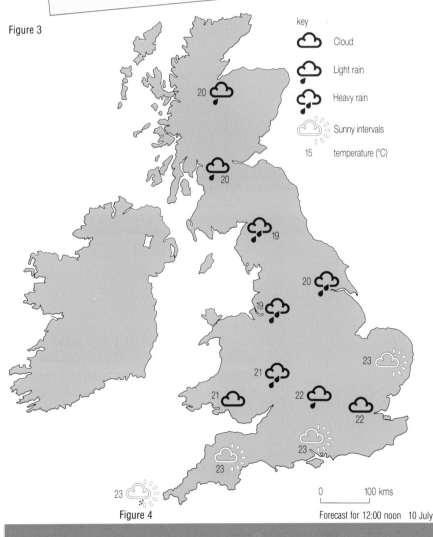

key
- Cloud
- Light rain
- Heavy rain
- Sunny intervals
- 15 temperature (°C)

Figure 4

Forecast for 12:00 noon 10 July

0   100 kms

Figure 2

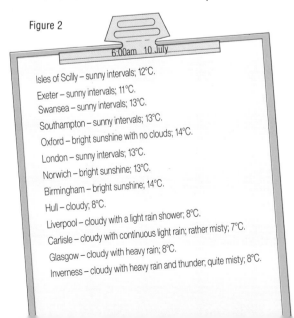

6:00am 10 July

Isles of Scilly – sunny intervals; 12°C.

Exeter – sunny intervals; 11°C.

Swansea – sunny intervals; 13°C.

Southampton – sunny intervals; 13°C.

Oxford – bright sunshine with no clouds; 14°C.

London – sunny intervals; 13°C.

Norwich – bright sunshine; 13°C.

Birmingham – bright sunshine; 14°C.

Hull – cloudy; 8°C.

Liverpool – cloudy with a light rain shower; 8°C.

Carlisle – cloudy with continuous light rain; rather misty; 7°C.

Glasgow – cloudy with heavy rain; 8°C.

Inverness – cloudy with heavy rain and thunder; quite misty; 8°C.

4.3 The effect of buildings on local climate

So far in this chapter we have looked at the day-to-day conditions of the atmosphere – this is what we mean by the **weather**. The average weather conditions over a long period of time form the **climate** of a place. We can talk about a particular climate covering a huge area, for example, the Arctic. We can also talk about local climates such as valleys, urban areas or even within a complex of buildings such as a school.

You can probably think of an area around your school that has a local climate. It may be a very breezy passageway between two buildings or it may be a tarmac quad that becomes a 'sun-trap' in the summer. Buildings can have quite an effect on winds and temperatures as the diagrams in Figure 1 show.

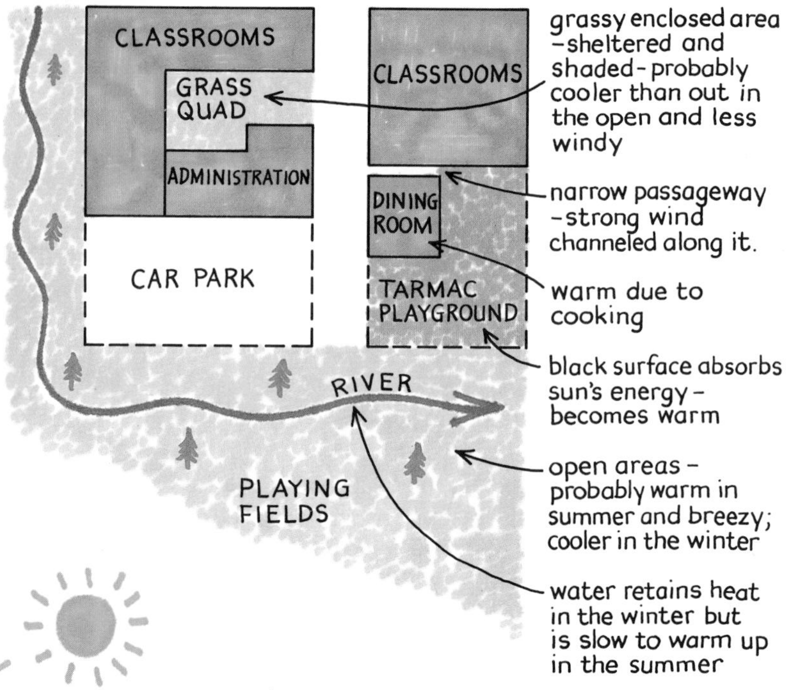
CLASSROOMS
GRASS QUAD
ADMINISTRATION
CAR PARK
CLASSROOMS
DINING ROOM
TARMAC PLAYGROUND
RIVER
PLAYING FIELDS
grassy enclosed area –sheltered and shaded-probably cooler than out in the open and less windy
narrow passageway -strong wind channeled along it.
warm due to cooking
black surface absorbs sun's energy - becomes warm
open areas - probably warm in summer and breezy; cooler in the winter
water retains heat in the winter but is slow to warm up in the summer

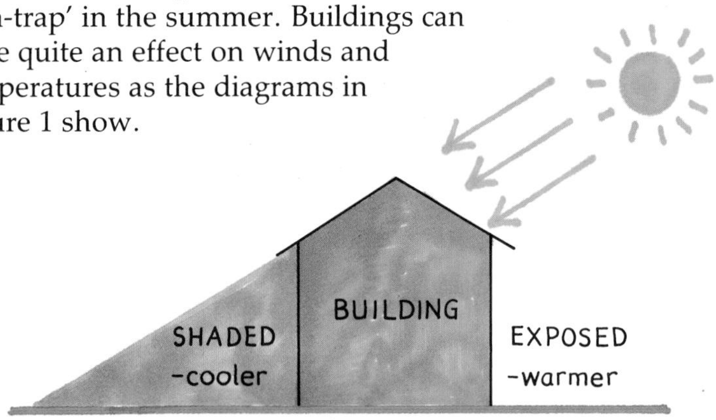
BUILDING
SHADED -cooler
EXPOSED -warmer

Figure 1

Activities

1 In this Activity your class is going to study the local climatic conditions around your school.

Data Collection

You will need a plan of the school grounds and instruments to measure temperature and wind, **whirling hygrometres** are good for measuring temperature. (They can also be used to measure **humidity** if you wanted to extend this Activity.) Wind is more difficult to measure – Figure 2 gives you some ideas.

In groups of 3 and 4, take measurements at selected sites around the school. It is important to choose as many different sites as you can including sites well away from buildings to act as 'controls'. Measurements should be taken at the same time to enable comparisons to be made. The most interesting results occur on clear frosty days or during a sunny morning. A low angled sun will best show the effects of open and shaded areas. A breeze is essential too!

1. <u>Beaufort Scale</u>

2. <u>Anemometer</u>
   Hand-held anemometers are available but are quite expensive.

3. <u>Wind displacement</u>

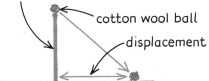

1 metre pole gives a standard height for release of cotton wool ball

cotton wool ball

displacement

A cotton wool ball can be released from a standard height. The horizontal distance that it is blown can be measured to where it <u>first</u> reaches the ground.
Direction of the wind can also be calculated.

Figure 2

4. <u>Ribbon/wool gauge</u>

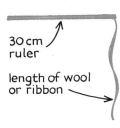

30 cm ruler

length of wool or ribbon

This simple equipment is excellent for measuring light breezes. The ruler should be held at arms-length and one of three values recorded : –

1 (calm)　　2　　3

Wind direction can also be calculated.

At each site, measurement should be taken of **temperature**, **wind speed/displacement**, and **wind direction** (remember that direction is where the wind has come from!)

Data Presentation
Each person needs to produce a table recording the results at each site. Lay a sheet of tracing paper over your base map and draw a small circle at each site. Now look at Figure 3 to see how to show the information at each site.

Figure 3

Data Analysis
Having completed your map, discuss with a friend what your map shows. Are there any areas that are particularly warm or cold? Why? Are there areas with particularly strong winds? Why? Is there any difference between grassy areas and tarmac areas? Why?

These are just some of the things you could look for. Don't forget always to try to explain the reasons for a pattern you have identified.

Colour the circle according to a series of temperature categories. Increase the darkness of the colour as temperature increases

Use a 'pointer' to show wind direction. It points in the direction from where the wind has come. The pointer could increase in thickness or length as wind speed increases, e.g. 1cm = 10cms displacement of cotton wool ball.

4.4 Measuring the weather

1 Temperature

The temperature of the air is measured with a **thermometer**. Figure 1 shows a **maximum-minimum thermometer**. This instrument records both the highest (maximum) and the lowest (minimum) temperature for a period of time, usually a day.

Temperature is usually given in **degrees celsius** (°C).

The difference between the daily maximum and the daily minimum is the **diurnal** (daily) **range**. So, for example:

Maximum temperature = 10°C
Minimum temperature = −2°C

Diurnal range = 12°C

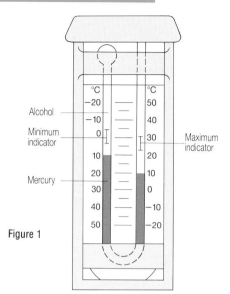

Figure 1

Activities

1 Study the thermometer readings in Figure 2. They show the temperatures recorded at the end of a 24 hour period.

  a Find the **maximum temperature, the minimum temperature** and the **diurnal range** for each. Present your answers in a table.

  b For each one, suggest the likely time of year:
    ● summer   ● winter   ● spring/autumn.

2 Figure 3 plots the results of temperature readings taken for a week in March, Figure 4 shows how these figures can be plotted onto a graph.

  a Make a copy of Figure 4 and complete the graph. Join the **maximum** points with a red line and the **minimum** points with a blue line. Shade the area between the two lines – label it the **diurnal range**. Give your graph a title and remember to label the axes.

  b Which day had the highest temperature and what was it?

  c On how many days was there a frost?

  d What was the diurnal range on Thursday?

  e When was the greatest diurnal range?

  f Work out the average **maximum** temperature for the week. To do this, add up all the maximum temperatures and divide by the number of days.

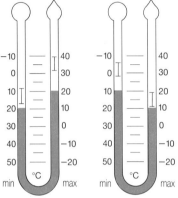

The temperature is read at the base of each indicator. The maximum temperature in the above example is 22°C and the minimum temperature is 5°C.

Figure 2

Figure 3

	Monday	Tuesday	Wednesday	Thursday	Friday	Saturday	Sunday
Maximum	10	10	5	4	6	3	4
Minimum	3	1	−3	−2	0	0	1

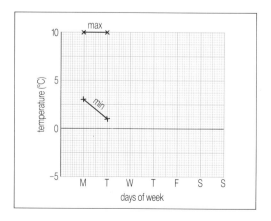

Figure 4

2 Precipitation

Precipitation is the name given to any moisture deposited on the ground. So, it includes rain, snow, sleet, dew, and so on. In Britain, most precipitation falls as rain (see Figure 5).

Look at Figure 6. It shows the **water cycle** and explains how rain is formed.

Precipitaton is measured using a **rain gauge**. Water passes through a funnel and collects in the bottom of a collecting jar. At the end of each day, the jar of water is poured into a measuring container (like a test tube) and the amount of precipitation can be discovered. The units of measurement are **millimetres**.

Figure 5

Figure 6

Air cools as it rises
Water vapour CONDENSES to form clouds

PRECIPITATION falls from clouds

EVAPORATION of water from the ground surface

Lakes

Lakes

Rivers

Rivers

Rivers

Oceans

Figure 6

Activities

Figure 7

3 a Make a copy of the **water cycle** Figure 6.
  b Copy the following sentences filling in the gaps with the correct words. Use your diagram to help you.

  Precipitation most commonly takes the form of .... Once on the ground, it may pass into rivers, ... , and .... Water is then .... into the air as water vapour. As the air cools, the water vapour may .... to form .... These clouds may then give precipitation so completing the ....

4 Study Figure 7. It shows a simple **rain gauge**. Unfortunately, the artist wasn't concentrating properly when drawing the diagram and some of the labels have been wrongly placed!

  Make a copy of Figure 7 putting the labels in their correct places. Be careful, as not all labels have been wrongly positioned!

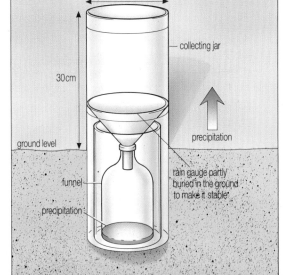

13cm

30cm

collecting jar

precipitation

ground level

funnel

precipitation

rain gauge partly buried in the ground to make it stable

5 Project: Keeping a weather log

Look at Figure 8. It is a **weather log**. On a copy of the log you can record the weather for a period of a week (or longer if you wish). Figure 9 contains some information to help you with the completion of the log.

Your teacher may decide to change the log slightly depending on what measuring equipment your school has available.

When your log has been completed do the following:

a Make a neat copy of the log. Use symbols if you wish to show the different types of weather recorded (don't forget to include a key!).

b Show some of the information in diagram form. Figure 10 shows some of the diagrams you could draw.

c Write a summary of the weather experienced during the week.

Figure 8

	temperature		precipitation				cloud cover		wind direction		wind speed	
	minimum	maximum	type	duration	intensity	amount	am	pm	am	pm	am	pm
Monday												
Tuesday												
Wednesday												
Thursday												
Friday												
Saturday												
Sunday												

Figure 9

1 Temperature

Record maximum and minimum termperature for the day. An alternative would be two present readings, am and pm.

2 Precipitation

Type	rain, snow, sleet, etc.
Duration	estimate the number of hours of precipitation
Intensity	estimate whether precipitation was heavy/moderate/light
Amount	total daily amount (if school has rain gauge)

3 Cloud Cover

Estimate the amount of cloud in the sky. Give in "eighths" (oktas) e.g. 4 oktas is a sky half covered with cloud.

4 Wind Direction

Estimate the wind direction. Use a wind vane, hand held ribbon, licked fingers, etc. Give wind direction to 8 points of the compass (see page 6). Wind direction is the direction *from where the wind has come*. Be careful.

5 Wind Speed

Use the Beaufort Scale (alongside) to estimate the wind force.

6 Other

Write any other interesting information e.g. "frost lasted all day"; "heavy thunderstorms during the night"; etc.

NB. When taking readings twice a day, always stick to the same times e.g. 10.00 am and 4.00 pm everyday.

Beaufort force	Type of wind	Effects to look for	Speed km/h
0	Calm	Smoke rises vertically	0
1	Light air	Smoke drifts	1–5
2	Light breeze	Wind felt on face, leaves rustle weather vanes move	6–11
3	Gentle breeze	Leaves and small twigs move, flags extended	12–2
4	Moderate beeze	Dust and loose paper blow about, small branches move	21–3
5	Fresh breeze	Small trees sway, wavelets form on water	31–4
6	Strong breeze	Large branches sway, umbrellas used with difficulty, telegraph wires whistle	41–5
7	Moderate gale	Whole trees sway, hard to walk into the wind	51–6
8	Gale	Twigs break off trees, very hard to walk into the wind	61–7
9	Strong gale	Chimney pots and slates blow off	75–8
10	Storm	Trees uprooted, serious damage to buildings	88–10
11	Violent storm	Rarely occurs inland, causes widespread damage	101–1
12	Hurricane	Disastrous results	115–

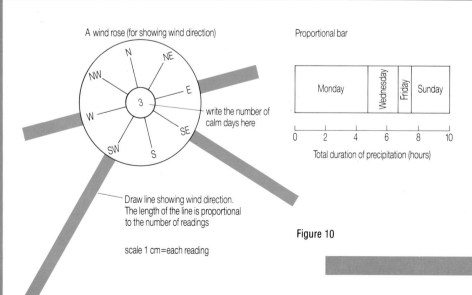

A wind rose (for showing wind direction)

3

write the number of calm days here

Draw line showing wind direction. The length of the line is proportional to the number of readings

scale 1 cm=each reading

Proportional bar

Monday   Wednesday   Friday   Sunday

0   2   4   6   8   10

Total duration of precipitation (hours)

Figure 10

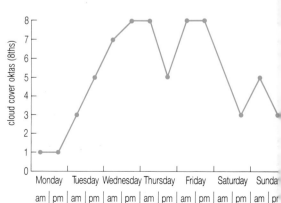

Line graph

cloud cover oktas (8ths)

Monday   Tuesday   Wednesday   Thursday   Friday   Saturday   Sunday

am | pm | am | pm | am | pm | am | pm | am | pm | am | pm | am | pm

3 The Stevenson Screen

Your school probably has a **Stevenson Screen** (Figure 11). This large white box houses weather instruments. It is important as a safe home for the thermometer as it allows air to pass through it but keeps the instrument in the shade.

Figure 11

sloping roof

white colour to reflect the sun

wooden slatted sides

legs keep screen off the ground

door closes and can be locked

situated in an open space

4.5 Acid Rain

Figure 1 shows that the **pH scale** runs from 1 (acid) – 14 (alkaline). Remember there is a ten-fold increase between one pH value and the next.

Normal rainwater is already slightly acidic (see Figure 1). This is because it picks up CO_2 from the atmosphere as it falls. However, in many industrial parts of the world it is even more acidic – true **acid rain**.

Acid rain can have a pH as low as 3; anything less than 4 will harm sensitive plants. Increased acidity is explained in Figure 2. There is much evidence that acid rain has damaged forests and killed fish in lakes and rivers.

One of the most important factors affecting acid rain damage is the wind direction. In Britain the **prevailing** (dominant) wind is from the south-west. This means that areas to the north-east of industrial regions are likely to suffer most from acid rain.

Figure 1 pH scale

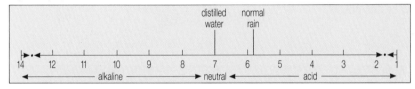

Figure 2 The formation of acid rain

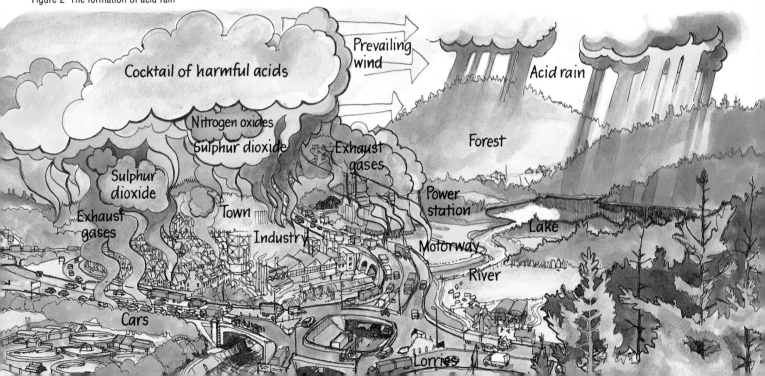

Activities

1 Make a copy of the pH scale in Figure 1. Add the various drawings in Figure 3 against their correct pH values.

2 Carry out your own study of acid rain.
 a Each member of the class needs to collect a sample of rain and test its acidity using narrow range (pH 4.5–7.5) indicator paper – your science department will have some.
 b Make a note of the wind direction that brought the rain.
 c The values can then be plotted onto a map of your home area using a range of colours from light to dark as pH decreases.
 d Describe any patterns shown by your map. Is there any difference between rural and urban areas? If there is heavy industry or a power station in your area, see whether it has had any effect on the results of your survey.

3 One major way of reducing acid rain is to reduce the emissions of harmful gases from power stations. This would lead to an increase in the cost of electricity. Discuss in small groups the advantages and disadvantages of this policy.

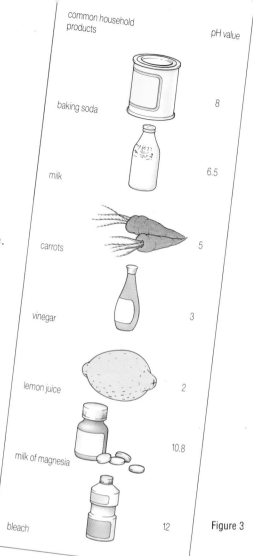

common household products — pH value

baking soda — 8
milk — 6.5
carrots — 5
vinegar — 3
lemon juice — 2
milk of magnesia — 10.8
bleach — 12

Figure 3

Dictionary

acid rain   rainwater made acidic by gases emitted from human activity.
Beaufort Scale   scale from 1–12 used to measure **wind** strength.
climate   long term general conditions of the atmosphere averaged over many years for an area or region of the world.
condensation   process where water vapour becomes water liquid. This occurs when air cools and becomes saturated.
diurnal range   daily variation, usually in temperature.

evaporation   process where water liquid becomes water vapour. In this way, water passes from the earth's surface to the atmosphere.
precipitation   all forms of moisture deposited on the ground. Includes rain, snow (ice crystals), sleet (mixture of rain and snow), etc.
prevailing wind   dominant (most common) wind direction. In Britain, it is from a SW direction.

rain gauge   instrument used to measure precipitation.
Stevenson Screen   white box on legs used to house weather instruments.
thermometer   instrument used to measure temperature.
weather   day to day conditions of the atmosphere including temperature, and precipitation values.
wind rose   diagram used to show wind direction.

5 Resources and Energy

When you got up this morning you went through a number of different activities like washing, getting dressed, having breakfast. All these use **resources**: water and soap for washing; wool, cotton, nylon in your clothes; and food (perhaps cereals) for your breakfast. Even as you are reading this you are using resources: what is the chair on which you are sitting made from? Paper, made from wood, is used for this textbook. A resource helps us make things and do things.

Many resources are metals and minerals from rocks like iron ore (which is used to make steel) and sand (used to make glass). Others, like coal, oil, and gas, are **energy** resources which provide us with fuel and power. Some resources cannot be replaced once we have used them up: these are called **non-renewable** resources. The amount we know can be used is called a **reserve**. For example, Britain has enough coal reserves to last over two hundred years and enough gas in the bed of the North Sea to last well into the next century (provided we do not increase the rate at which we are using them.) Fortunately many non-renewable resources can be **recycled**. Your school may have collected old newspapers to be recycled into paper and cardboard. A lot of the world's steel is made from scrap, recycled from old car bodies, disused machinery and so on.

Some natural resources can be used over and over again. If we are careful with their use, they are unlikely to run out. Water from rivers, the wind, sunlight, trees and crops are all examples of what are called **renewable** resources.

Activities

1 a Figure 1 shows some of the resources that may be used in a typical house. Study it carefully and then list the resources used by the house and its occupants. List the resources under the headings shown here:

   non-renewable   renewable   energy

  b Add to the three lists other resources which your house contains. Write these in a different colour.

Figure 1

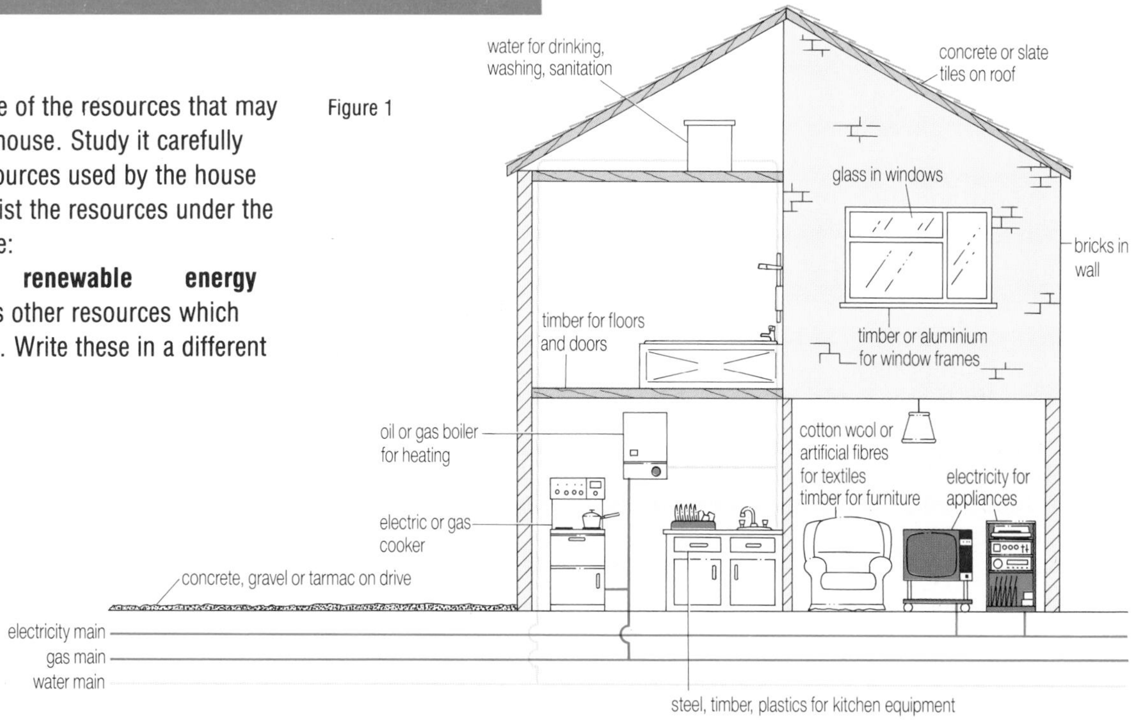

water for drinking, washing, sanitation

concrete or slate tiles on roof

glass in windows

bricks in wall

timber for floors and doors

timber or aluminium for window frames

oil or gas boiler for heating

cotton wool or artificial fibres for textiles
timber for furniture

electricity for appliances

electric or gas cooker

concrete, gravel or tarmac on drive

electricity main
gas main
water main

steel, timber, plastics for kitchen equipment

2 Look carefully at Figure 2. This shows some of the major resources to be found in Britain.

 a Make a copy of Figure 2. Complete the key by writing in the name of the county or counties in the empty spaces provided. You may need to use your atlas!

 b For each of the resources shown, write down its major uses and say whether it is **renewable** or **non-renewable**.

3 Try to find as many examples as you can of things that have been made from **recycled** resources. What is being done in your home area to encourage the recycling of materials like paper and glass?

Figure 2

key

resource	counties	resource	counties
⊗ hydro-electricity		■ limestone and chalk	
coal		□ gravel	
● oil		▲ china clay	
⊙ natural gas		‡‡ forest	
△ salt		water from rivers	

5.2 Water resources

In Britain only a very small proportion of our water is used for domestic supply. Most is used in industry particularly for cooling, for example in power stations. Industries smelting metals, processing foods or making paper use vast quantities of water. Farming too depends on water for watering livestock or irrigating crops.

Water in the UK comes from three sources (see Figure 1):–

● **Reservoirs**. Some are natural but most have been made, often by damming an upland river valley. For example, a number of reservoirs in Wales are vital sources of water for Liverpool and Birmingham.

● **Rivers**. Most water is taken from rivers. It is treated before being piped to industries and homes. Once used, the water is treated before going back into a river. In this way pollution is controlled.

● **Aquifers**. In some parts of the UK, e.g. South East England, water is pumped from underground reservoirs called **aquifers**. Aquifers occur where water is able to pass through and be stored in rocks which contain air spaces called **pores**. Such rocks are **permeable**. Those containing a lot of pores are said to be **porous**. Sandstone and chalk are both permeable and porous – they make excellent aquifers.

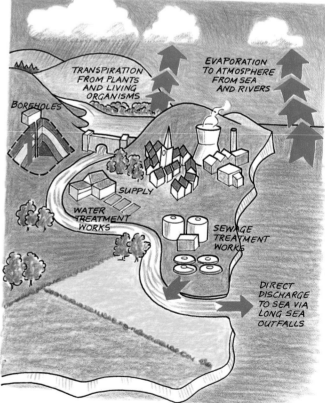

Figure 1

Sometimes water has to be transferred from one part of the country to another. In Britain most rain falls in the north and west yet most demand for water is in the east and south. Pipelines and artificial channels are used to move water towards areas of greatest demand.

Water is supplied to our homes by the water authorities. These are regulated by the National Rivers Authority. The NRA comprises 10 regions (see Figure 2) and has responsibility for flood protection, management of fisheries and control of water quality.

Figure 2

10 National Rivers Authority Regions

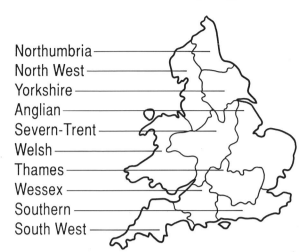

Northumbria
North West
Yorkshire
Anglian
Severn-Trent
Welsh
Thames
Wessex
Southern
South West

Activities

1 Draw a poster illustrating the importance of water. You could include sketches or photographs from magazines. Try to show the great range of uses for water.

2 a Make a copy of Figure 1. Use the information in the text to add labels to the diagram and draw arrows to show the movement of water.

   b Do you think the water supply industry can be called a 'cycle'? Explain your answer.

3 Study Figure 1 on page 38 which shows a reservoir in an upland area. Discuss with a friend why upland valleys are often good places for reservoirs. Now try to list some of the possible problems with flooding an upland valley to form a reservoir.

4 During times of water shortage (see Figure 3 page 23) the public is banned from using hoses. Suggest other ways that water could be conserved in the home.

5 Carry out some research into water supply in your Rivers Authority Region to discover your sources of water. You could use local libraries and maps in atlases to show rainfall amounts, rivers, reservoirs and aquifers.

5.3 Energy Resources

If you look back at Figure 1 in unit 5.1, on page 33, you will see that the house uses **energy**. Energy gives us the power to do things and to make things work. Figure 1 shows the percentage of each energy source used in British homes.

Britain is in the fortunate position of being **self-sufficient** in energy. This is mostly because of our North Sea Oil and gas reserves. In fact we actually export oil to other countries. However, unless new fields are found, North Sea oil and gas will start to run out early next century. After that we may begin to consume more than we produce.

Apart from using them up, cutting down on the amount of energy we use will also help to reduce pollution. Gas, coal and oil are **fossil fuels**. When these are burnt, **carbon dioxide** is given off. This gas absorbs heat which may raise the temperature of the atmosphere. This is known as the **greenhouse effect**. Exhaust gases from vehicles also contribute to **smog**, and are dangerous to our health.

Figure 1:
Major Sources of Energy used in British Homes

Gas	45%
Coal	26%
Electricity	20%
Oil	9%

Activities

1 Study Figure 1
   a Draw a pie chart to show the figures.
   b Name the energy source in each of the photographs in Figure 2.
      Don't forget to give your chart a title and key.

2 In what ways do think your own home's energy sources are different from those shown in Figure 1?

3 Design a poster to encourage people to use less energy in the home.

4 Do you think that your school wastes energy? Suggest ways in which it could save energy.

A

B

Figure 2

C

5.4   Electricity

Electricity is the most convenient and widely used source of energy (see Figure 1). It is instantly available at the flick of a switch! Although it is clean and efficient to use in the home and in the factory, it is not always clean and efficient to generate. Figure 2 shows how other energy sources are used to generate electricity.

Figure 1

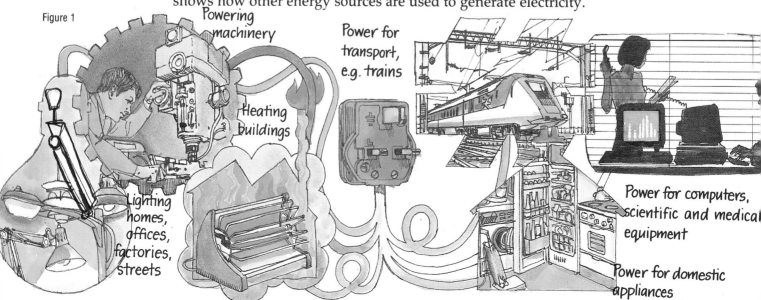

Powering machinery

Power for transport, e.g. trains

Heating buildings

Lighting homes, offices, factories, streets

Power for computers, scientific and medical equipment

Power for domestic appliances

Figure 2 Methods of generating electricity

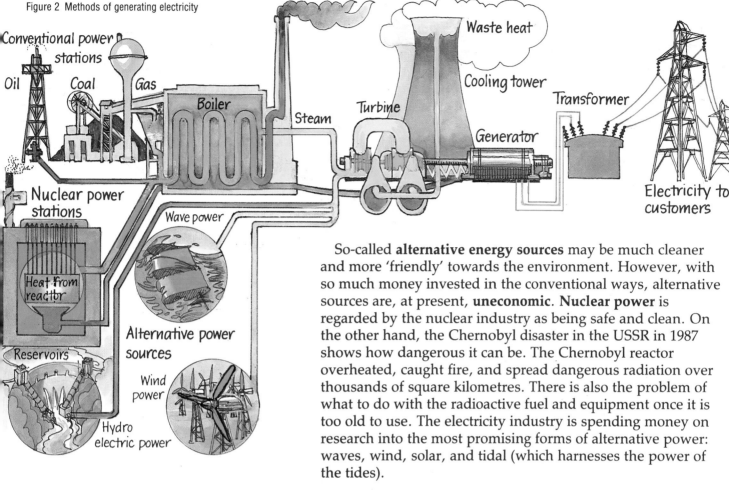

So-called **alternative energy sources** may be much cleaner and more 'friendly' towards the environment. However, with so much money invested in the conventional ways, alternative sources are, at present, **uneconomic**. **Nuclear power** is regarded by the nuclear industry as being safe and clean. On the other hand, the Chernobyl disaster in the USSR in 1987 shows how dangerous it can be. The Chernobyl reactor overheated, caught fire, and spread dangerous radiation over thousands of square kilometres. There is also the problem of what to do with the radioactive fuel and equipment once it is too old to use. The electricity industry is spending money on research into the most promising forms of alternative power: waves, wind, solar, and tidal (which harnesses the power of the tides).

Activities

1 Figure 1 shows the major uses for electricity. Make your own list of all the ways in which you and your family use electricity in one week.

2 Study the ways in which electricity is generated in Figure 2. Now write out the following paragraph filling in the gaps with the correct words from the diagram.

_____ power stations produce heat from burning coal, gas and _____ . The steam drives the _____ which turns the generator to produce the _____ . The steam condenses back into water in the _____ _____ . Up to 40% of the total energy is wasted from here and from the _____ . An alternative way of driving the _____ is to use water power from a reservoir. This is called _____ _____ _____ . _____ power and _____ power can also be used.

3 The map in Figure 3 shows the distribution of nuclear power stations in Britain.
  a What reasons can you think of to explain why they are all on or near the coast?
  b Use an atlas to discover how many are located in or close to towns and cities. Try to explain your findings.

Figure 3

4 Figure 4 is a photograph of an alternative way of producing electricity.
  a How do you think the electricity is being produced?
  b Describe the relief of the area. How do you think that the nature of the relief assists the method of generation?
  c Describe the advantages and disadvantages of this method.

Figure 4

5.5   Case Study: The Rheidol HEP Scheme in mid-Wales

You discovered in the last unit that water power can drive a turbine to generate electricity. This is known as **Hydro Electric Power** (HEP). The Rheidol Scheme in mid-Wales is an important one and works like this.

1 The upper course of the Afon Rheidol river is dammed at the Nant-y-Moch Reservoir (see Figure 1).

2 An underground pipeline carries water down to the Dinas Power Station which can produce 12 000 kilowatts of electricity (enough to run 12 000 single bar electric fires).

3 Water from a second reservoir at Dinas is piped underground and down to the main station at Cwm Rheidol. This can generate 40 000 kilowatts.

Figure 1

4 The Cwm Rheidol Reservoir has been formed to regulate the flow of water downstream in the Afon Rheidol river. This can prevent flooding in times of heavy rain.

5 The electricity can be directed to both North and South Wales when needed.

The landscape of mid-Wales is very suitable for the production of HEP. The high ground provides steep slopes for the powerful flow of water. Steep sided valleys are a convenient shape for forming reservoirs, and heavy rainfall from the hills around keeps the reservoirs full. The area from which the water is collected is called the **catchment area**.

Activities

1 Figure 1 is a photograph of the Nant-y-moch Reservoir and dam. Sketch this in your exercise book and add the following labels: dam; reservoir; catchment area; Afon Rheidol.

2 Make a copy of the map in Figure 2. Use the text and Figure 3 to help you to do the following:
  a In the correct boxes write down:
   Nant-y-Moch Reservoir;   Dinas Reservoir;   Cwm Rheidol Reservoir.
  b Label the Afon Rheidol.
  c Name, in their correct positions, the two power stations which are marked on the map with a cross.
  d Draw with straight lines the approximate paths of the pipelines.

3 Why do you think that the pipelines have been put underground?

4 Turn back to Chapter 5.3 and explain why HEP stations:
  a do not pollute the atmosphere, and
  b are using a **renewable resource**.

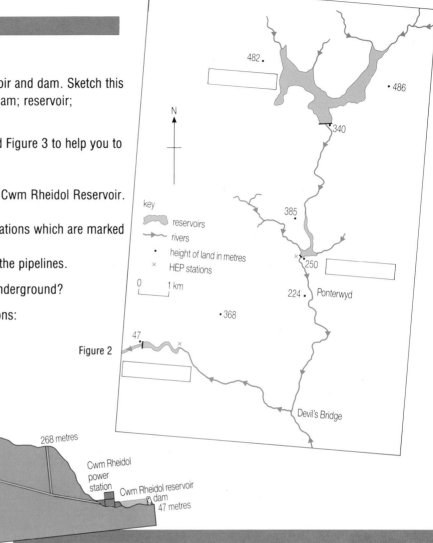

Figure 2

Figure 3

Dictionary

alternative energy energy sources other than gas, oil and coal.

carbon dioxide a gas given off when fossil fuels are burned.

catchment area an area around a reservoir that collects rainwater.

energy the ability to do work.

fossil-fuels fuels that come from fossilised materials coal, gas and oil.

greenhouse effect the possible warming of the atmosphere mostly caused by the increase of carbon dioxide in the atmosphere.

hydro electric power electricity generated by running water.

mineral veins veins in rock containing mineral ores.

non-renewable resources that cannot be used more than once.

nuclear power heat produced from a nuclear reactor used to generate electricity.

recycled material that has been used again e.g. glass from old bottles.

renewable resources that can be used over and over again e.g. water.

resources materials that are used to make things.

self-sufficient the supply of something without outside help.

smog combination of fog and pollutants like smoke.

uneconomic an activity that will not produce a profit or a good return on investment.

6 Population

Figure 1 is a recent photograph of a family. Compare it with Figure 2 which is a family shot taken in 1915.

In Figure 1 the family is made up of Mr and Mrs Clarke, their two children Louise and Annie, Mrs Clarke's mother and the dog, Leo. Mr and Mrs Clarke form a **generation** and their children form another generation.

Mrs Clarke's mother was only a young girl when the photograph in Figure 2 was taken. She appears with her two sisters, brother, her parents and an uncle.

Families today are smaller than they used to be – many of you probably only have one or two brothers and sisters (**siblings**) whereas your grandparents probably had four or more.

Figure 1

Figure 2

Activities

1 Carry out a survey as a class into changing family size.
  a To do this each member of your class needs to find out the following:
   - The number of children in your family, including yourself
   - The number of each of your parent's brothers and sisters, including themselves
   - The number of each of your grandparent's brothers and sisters, including themselves
  b Copy and complete the table in Figure 3 to record your results. The information can be pooled together for the whole class.

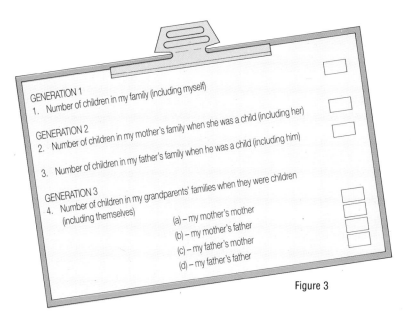

Figure 3

c Combine the results for the whole class and work out an average family size for each of the three generations.
d Produce a bar graph to show your results.
e Is it true that family size has gradually decreased over the years? Discuss as a class why this has happened. It would be interesting to ask parents and grandparents why larger families were common in the past.

2 a What do you understand by the 'generation gap'?
b Give some examples of the way in which the 'generation gap' shows itself in everyday life.
c Why do you think there is a 'generation gap'?
d What could be done to close the 'gap'?

6.2 The Population Census

In 1991 your parents will have completed the most recent population **census** – you may have seen it. The census is simply a population count taken on one night every 10 years – the last one was carried out in 1981 and the next will be in 2001.

Over the decades it has become more and more detailed and now there are many questions which have to be answered by each **head of household**. Figure 1 shows part of the 1991 census and Figure 2 lists some of the other details asked for. It is really just a form of **questionnaire**, which is something you have already come across.

One important thing about the census is that the names of people are kept a secret for 100 years. Although the information can be used, it cannot be linked to individuals.

Most countries of the world have a census every 10 years to discover the social and economic characteristics of their population.

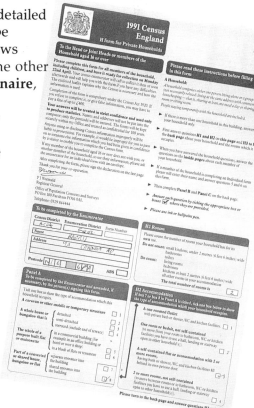

Figure 1

Figure 2

1. Date of birth of each person in house
2. Marital status
3. Relationship in household
4. Address
5. Address one year ago
6. Country of birth
7. Employment details
8. Place of work
9. Journey to work
10. Qualifications

Activities

1 Discuss in pairs or in small groups why you think there is a need for a regular census (hint: think of plans that might need to be made to cater for the elderly or the very young).

2 Do you think it is important to keep people's identity a secret for 100 years? Why?

3 a Make up a questionnaire to discover some **social trends** of the people in your class. Figure 3 suggests a few questions you might like to ask. Notice how the questions concern social habits such as what you do in your spare time. Just like a census, there are several options for answers. This makes it easy to analyse the data. Discuss as a class what questions you want to include.

b Each member of the class should then complete the questionnaire and return it unnamed (just like the census) to your teacher. Your teacher will then collate the information.

It is important that everybody's identity remains anonymous.

c Once the information has been pooled, you can draw graphs to illustrate the information and write a few sentences about each. Are the results surprising?

Akash: 'Where did you used to live in India?'

Mrs. Soni: 'I used to live in a small town called Merut near New Delhi.'

Akash: 'Did you go to school there?'

Mrs. Soni: 'Yes, I went to an English convent school called St. Marys.'

Akash: 'What did you do when you finished studying?'

Mrs. Soni: 'I took up a job as a school teacher. In India, teachers are still allowed to cane children although I would never do that. Schools are not as well disciplined as they are in England.'

Akash: 'Is there anything unusual about the people in India?'

Mrs. Soni: 'Of course not! They're humans as well, aren't they?'

Akash: 'How many were you in your family?'

Mrs. Soni 'My mother and father and my older brother and sister.'

Akash: 'What did your father do?'

Mrs. Soni: 'He was in the army.'

Akash: 'Do you prefer living in London to living in Merut?'

Mrs. Soni: 'In some ways I would prefer to be back in India, although I want my children to be educated in English schools'

Figure 4

Figure 3

1. What is your age? --------
2. Do you have a computer at home? Yes --- No ---
3. If 'yes', what make is it? --------
4. Do you have any pets? Yes --- No ---
5. If 'yes', what pets have you and how many? Dog ----------- Cat ----------- Fish ----------- Bird ----------- Hampster ------ Others ----------------------------------
6. Approximately how many hours of television do you watch on a typical weekday evening -------- hours; weekend evening -------- hours
7. Which channel do you watch most often? BBC1 ------ BBC2 ------ ITV ---------- C4 ---------- Other --------
8. Do you have a satellite dish at home? Yes --- No ---
9. What do you most often have for breakfast? Cereal only ------ Toast only ------ Cereal and toast ------ Cooked meal ------ Drink only ------ Nothing ------
10. How much pocket money do you get a week? <£1 ----------- £1-£2 ---------- £2-3 ---------- £3-5 ---------- £5+ -----------
11. What is your favourite hobby or interest? -------------------
12. Where did you spend your main family holidy last year? At home ------ Britain ------ Europe ------ Elsewhere ------

4 Carry out an interview with a relative or friend who is of a different generation or background from yourself. For an older relative, find out what life was like when they were your age. What did they do without the television? What was the war really like? What was school like? What did they do for their summer holiday? These are just some of the questions you could ask – there are many more you can make up for yourself.

You might like to do an interview with someone who has lived or who is living in a different country. Figure 4 is an interview carried out by a boy who talked to his Indian mother. Find out what life is like in the country concerned.

You may wish to tape your interview or even to video it.

Write up your interview and consider how you would have felt about living at the time or in the country of the person you have interviewed.

6.3   Population density

People are not spread evenly in the United Kingdom. They tend to be concentrated in urban and industrial areas with relatively few people living in remote country areas. About 80 per cent of us live in towns and cities. This is because most jobs are found here. There are also shops and leisure facilities. However, some people prefer to live in more pleasant country areas and travel to work in towns (**commute**).

The 'spread' of people can be examined using **population densities**. These figures tell us the number of people in a given area of land, usually 1 hectare or 1 square kilometre. Highest densities are found in towns and lowest densities in the countryside.

Activities

1 a Make an enlarged copy of your home **region** using the map in unit 2.1, Figure 3 (p. 13). Mark on the outlines of the **counties** in your region. This is going to be your base map.

b Figure 1 contains population density data. Use this information and the suggested colour key to colour your map correctly. It is important to try and use the colours suggested as they blend into one another gradually becoming darker as density increases. This type of map is called a **choropleth map**.

c Complete your map by doing the following:
- give your map a title including the word 'choropleth'
- add a key
- write the names of the counties
- locate your home city, town or village. You can locate other towns and cities if you wish.

d In a few sentences describe the pattern of population density. Is it evenly spread or are some areas more densely populated than others? Suggest some possible causes for density varying in your region.

Population densities (per hectare)

NORTH 2.0	**SOUTH EAST 6.4**	**WEST MIDLANDS 4.0**
Cleveland 9.5	Bedfordshire 4.3	Hereford and Worcester 1.7
Cumbria 0.7	Berkshire 5.9	Shropshire 1.1
Durham 2.4	Buckinghamshire 3.3	Staffordshire 3.8
Northumberland 0.6	East Sussex 4.0	Warwickshire 2.4
Tyne and Wear 20.9	Essex 4.2	West Midlands 29.1
	Greater London 42.6	
YORKSHIRE AND HUMBERSIDE 3.2	Hampshire 4.1	**NORTH WEST 8.7**
Humberside 2.4	Hertfordshire 6.0	Cheshire 4.1
North Yorkshire 0.9	Isle of Wight 3.4	Greater Manchester 20.0
South Yorkshire 8.3	Kent 4.1	Lancashire 4.5
West Yorkshire 10.1	Oxfordshire 2.2	Merseyside 22.2
	Surrey 6.0	
EAST MIDLANDS 2.5	West Sussex 3.5	**WALES 1.4**
Derbyshire 3.5		Clwyd 1.7
Leicestershire 3.5	**SOUTH WEST 1.9**	Dyfed 0.6
Lincolnshire 1.0	Avon 7.1	Gwent 3.2
Northamptonshire 2.4	Cornwall and Isles of Scilly 1.3	Gwynedd 0.6
Nottinghamshire 4.7	Devon 1.5	Mid Glamorgan 5.3
	Dorset 2.5	Powys 0.2
EAST ANGLIA 1.6	Gloucestershire 2.0	South Glamorgan 9.7
Cambridgeshire 1.9	Somerset 1.3	West Glamorgan 4.4
Norfolk 1.4	Wiltshire 1.6	
Suffolk 1.7		

Figure 1

Region	Yellow	Orange	Red	Brown	Black
		5.1 – 10	10.1 – 15	15.1 – 20	20.1+
NORTH	0 – 5.0	2.1 – 4.0	4.1 – 6.0	6.1 – 8.0	8.1 – 10.0
YORKS & HUMBERSIDE	0 – 2.0	1.1 – 2.0	2.1 – 3.0	3.1 – 4.0	4.1 – 5.0
EAST MIDLANDS	0 – 1.0	1.3 – 1.4	1.5 – 1.6	1.7 – 1.8	1.9 – 2.0
EAST ANGLIA	1.0 – 1.2	2.1 – 4.0	4.1 – 6.0	6.1 – 8.0	8.1+
SOUTH EAST	0 – 2	1.6 – 2.0	2.1 – 2.5	2.6 – 3.0	3.1+
SOUTH WEST	1.0 – 1.5	2.1 – 3.0	3.1 – 4.0	4.1 – 5.0	5.1+
WEST MIDLANDS	1.0 – 2.0	5.1 – 10.0	10.1 – 15.0	15.1 – 20	20.1+
NORTH WEST	0 – 5.0	2.1 – 4.0	4.1 – 6.0	6.1 – 8.0	8.1 – 10.0
WALES	0 – 2.0				

Figure 2

6.4   The quality of our lives

There are many factors which influence the **quality** of our lives. These may include the homes we live in, the food we eat, whether or not we have a computer, our family and friends, and the amount of money we have. It is easy to think, perhaps, that we have the 'best' quality of life if we have many possessions, but what if we are ill or have no friends?

People think differently about what determines their quality of life. In Figure 1 there are the views of a few people of different ages. Each has been asked to describe the most important factors affecting the quality of their lives. It is important to remember that views are personal – there are no 'rights' and 'wrongs'!

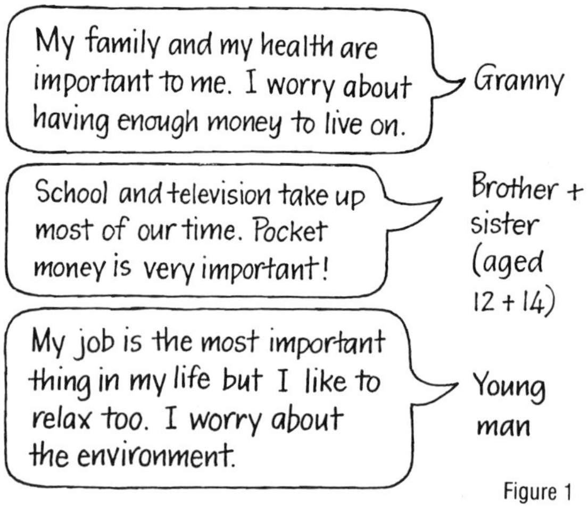

My family and my health are important to me. I worry about having enough money to live on. — Granny

School and television take up most of our time. Pocket money is very important! — Brother + sister (aged 12 + 14)

My job is the most important thing in my life but I like to relax too. I worry about the environment. — Young man

Figure 1

Activities

1 a Make a list in rough of as many factors as you can think of that affect the quality of your life. Now rank the top ten in order with the most important factor being number 1 and the least important being number 10.

b Listen to the top tens and the views of the others in your class. Now try to agree on a top ten for the whole class! This will not be easy!

One way to do this is to give points to the factors as follows:

1st ranked factor – 10 points
2nd ranked factor – 9 points
and so on.

Allocate points for all factors. The highest score will be then become the 1st ranked factor for the class; the second highest score, the 2nd ranked factor for the class; and so on.

Final scores could then be graphed as a series of bars.

Dictionary

census   count of people and a record of some of their characteristics
commute   travelling to work

generation   people born at about the same time, e.g. brothers and sisters within a family
generation gap   difference in values and ways of life between people of different generations

population density   numbers of people in a area, e.g. a hectare or square km.

7 *Settlement*

Those of you who live near London may refer to it as 'town'. Most of us, however, would consider London far too big to be a 'town'!

Look at Figure 1. It defines the common **types** of settlement. Notice how, as a settlement gets larger, it tends to offer more **functions** such as shops and recreation facilities. (Chapter 7.4 looks at shopping in more detail.)

It is possible to identify the types of settlements given in Figure 1 on Ordnance Survey maps. Turn to the map extract on page 108. The largest settlement on the map is Chester. It is a **city** as it has a population over 100 000 and it also has a cathedral. There are no **towns** on the map but there are a few **villages**, such as Eccleston (Figure 2) and Christleton (see Chapter 7.2). Find these on the extract and give their four – figure grid reference. Notice that, although they are both 'villages', Christleton is clearly larger than Eccleston. It also has more functions. There are several small **hamlets** such as Picton (4371—see Figure 3).

Settlements change over time. The village of Christleton, for example, has grown rapidly over the last few years – it is a **commuter** village with many of its residents working in nearby Chester. Eccleston, on the other hand, is mostly owned by the Duke of Westminster and it has remained almost unchanged for a very long time.

Sometimes settlements are abandoned. Many small villages in Wales grew up as mining villages during the 18th century but, as the mineral veins became exhausted, so the villages declined. Salem (see Figure 4) is an example of such a village.

Settlement type	Characteristics
Hamlet	A small cluster of houses, usually no facilities such as shops. Possibly a church.
Village	Villages vary in size. Large villages have a population of a few thousand and have a selection of shops, churches, a village hall, a primary school etc.
Town	Towns have populations of several tens of thousands. They will have many shops including supermarkets **chain stores** (e.g. Boots, W H Smith). They may have a railway station
City	A city has a population over 100 000 people, except some 'cathedral cities' which are smaller. Cities have large shopping centres, sports grounds, a railway station and possibly an airport.

key
- ■ house
- ✝ church
- S shop
- PH public house
- P post office
- ▢ built-up area

Figure 1

Figure 2

Figure 3

Figure 4

Activities

1 Work in pairs to make a list of **villages** and **hamlets** on the map extract (page 108) not already mentioned in this Chapter.

2 Carefully draw two sketches to compare the settlements of Picton (4371) and Saighton (4462). Try to draw your sketches to the same scale to allow comparison but do *not* trace them.

Show the houses/built-up area and mark on any facilities such as churches. Give each sketch a label stating what type of settlement it is.

3 Study your local map extract. Try to identify different types of settlement and draw sketches to compare them.

The city of Chester

Chester is one of Britain's oldest cities. It has its origins over 2000 years ago and was a Roman settlement in 79AD. During the 10th century it became a **fortified town** and its famous walls were built – part of the City Walls remain today. During the Middle Ages, Chester became an important **market town** and it was a port for the export of candles, salt and cheese.

Today, with a population of 116 000 it is one of the major cities in north-west England. It is a working city with industrial estates and factories (see Chapter 10.5) and an administrative centre – it is the 'County Town' of Cheshire. Chester is an important tourist centre with its famous 'rows' (Figure 5), historic buildings, cathedral, City Walls and the canal.

Look closely at Figure 6. It is an extract from the Chester Guide showing part of the city centre. Notice that much of the centre is **pedestrianised**. Nowadays most towns and cities have **pedestrian precincts** so that people can move safely between shops. Has your local town got one?

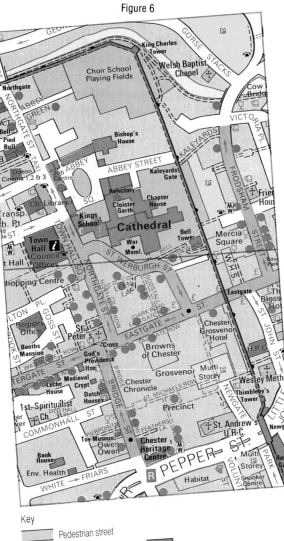

Figure 6

Key

Pedestrian street

Restaurant

Theatre/Cinema

Church

Local/National Government buildings

Place of interest

Station

Car park

Parks/gardens

Figure 5

Activities

4 Figure 7 is an aerial photograph of Chester city centre. It shows part of the area shown in Figure 6. Use Figure 6 to identify the features labelled on Figure 7.

5 Study Figure 6.
  a On the corner of which two roads is St. Andrew's Church?
  b On what road is 'Browns of Chester'?
  c Your car is parked at Newgate multi-storey car park. Describe a circular route that would take you to the cathedral, the Toy Museum and Chester Heritage Centre, returning to the car park.
  d How many restaurants are there on the map?
  e What evidence is there on the map to suggest that Chester Cathedral has a Choir School?
  f How many restaurants are there between Northgate and the Town Hall?
  g What do you think the R stands for in Pepper Street to the south of the map? Give reasons for your answer.

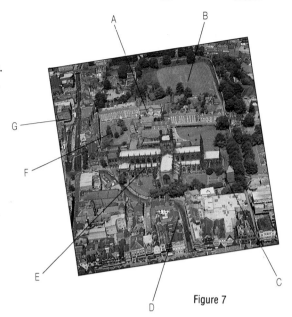

Figure 7

7.2 Studying villages

Most people in the UK live in towns and cities. To some of these people, villages are quiet and rather old fashioned with little going on. However, others may long for peace and quiet and a slower pace of life.

How correct are these **perceptions**? Ask people in your class who live in villages what life is really like. What are the advantages and disadvantages?

Up until quite recently, many villages declined as young people moved to the towns and cities. Local shops were forced to close (Figure 1) partly due to there being fewer people and partly because of the opening of large supermarkets in town and out-of-town locations which were able to charge lower prices. With fewer people in villages, public transport routes were cut. Many small railway stations closed and bus routes were reduced. Many villages became cut-off.

Figure 1

However, in the last 20 years, the trend has reversed. Most families now own a car. This means that they can live in rural areas and commute to work in towns. Villages close to urban areas have grown and new housing estates have been built. Despite this recent growth, these newcomers ('townies', as some villagers call them) can create problems. House prices in villages have risen as demand has increased – this has meant that some locals can no longer afford housing in their own village! The newcomers will probably shop in towns so village shops will not always benefit. Also, as they are car owners, there would be little chance of bus routes being re-introduced.

Activities

1 For this Activity you will need to work in pairs.

  a Draw up a list of the **advantages** and **disadvantages** of living in
  ● a town
  ● a village
  b Suggest reasons why a town family might wish to move to live in a village.
  c Imagine that your group works for the Community Services Department of a local authority.

A local parish council has asked for your help. Their village has become unpleasant and unfriendly in the last few years ever since a new housing estate has been built and several town families have moved in. There has been some vandalism on this estate by, they suspect, local village teenagers and this has led to a very unpleasant atmosphere in the village.

Your group has been asked to suggest ways in which the situation in the village can be improved. Make a list of your suggestions and discuss them with the rest of the class.

A village study: Christleton , Cheshire

Look at the OS map extract on page 108 and locate the village of Christleton. Notice that, in comparison with other villages on the map, it covers quite a large area. Just by looking at the map it is possible to tell that there is a school, a couple of churches and a Post Office. However, the map was drawn in 1986 so some of the functions may have changed. However, it is impossible to tell what the village is really like by just looking at the map. Therefore, you can see how important it is to go and see a village and study it at first-hand.

Christleton (pronounced 'Chrisleton') is a busy village with a population of just over 2 000. Figure 2 describes in map form and photographs some of the characteristics of the village.

Christleton is a very old village being mentioned in the Domesday Book of 1086 and it has an interesting mix of houses including large manors, medieval black and white cottages, large Victorian buildings and modern estates.

In terms of functions, Christleton has a Post Office/General Store, a hairdresser, a pub, a primary school and a secondary school, and two churches. There are several mobile services which come to the village once a week including bread, fish, greengrocer and library. There are three regular bus services which link the village with Chester.

Christleton is a thriving village with many clubs and societies. There is a Sports Centre (see Figure 2), built in 1972, which is used by the secondary school and the local community. It has facilities for squash, football, tennis and netball and it has an outdoor floodlit area. Christleton Sports Club (see Figure 2) runs football, cricket and hockey teams. There is a Womens' Institute, Cubs, Scouts and Brownies, a Bridge Club and a British Legion Club. Many of the clubs and societies meet in the Village Hall.

Christleton has a mixed economy. The biggest employer in the village is the Law College at Christleton Hall (see Figure 2). A lot of the students rent property in the village. A nursing home and several market gardens also provide employment for local people. A good many people also commute from the village to work in Chester.

There have been some recent changes. Two local shops, a butchers and the original village stores, have closed due to the opening of a large Sainsbury superstore less than 1 mile away at grid reference 430660. The local canal marina closed in 1986 and the buildings have been converted into flats.

Figure 2

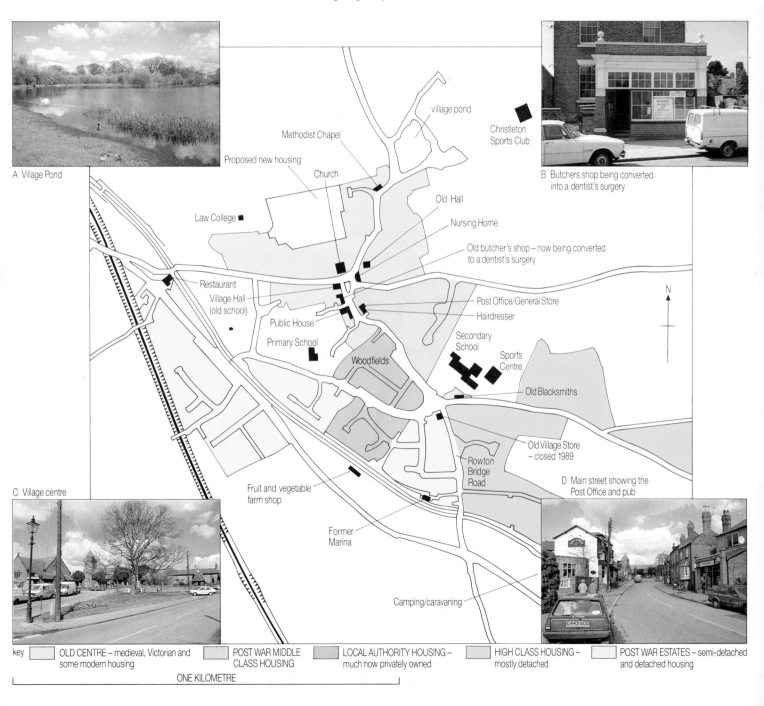

key | OLD CENTRE – medieval, Victorian and some modern housing | POST WAR MIDDLE CLASS HOUSING | LOCAL AUTHORITY HOUSING – much now privately owned | HIGH CLASS HOUSING – mostly detached | POST WAR ESTATES – semi-detached and detached housing

ONE KILOMETRE

Activities

2 Study Figure 2 and the information given in the text.

a Where do you think the centre of the village is? Give reasons for your answer.

b What is Christleton Hall used for?

c Why have two village shops recently had to close?

d How many bus services are there that link Christleton with Chester?

e What type of housing would you find at Woodfields?

f Imagine that you are the owner of a small hotel in Christleton — Old Hall Hotel (find Old Hall on Figure 2). You are about to write an advertising brochure which you will make available at the Chester Tourist Information Centre. The first page of your brochure needs to describe the attractions of the village of Christleton as a base for visitors to the area. Use the photographs in Figure 2 and other information in this section to design the front page of the brochure.

You should include the following:

● a sketch map of the area taken from the OS map extract on page 108. You must, for example, show where Christleton is in relation to Chester;

● a map of the village showing the location of Old Hall Hotel and other features and buildings that you think will be helpful and interesting;

● written information about the village suggesting walks and other things that visitors could see and do.

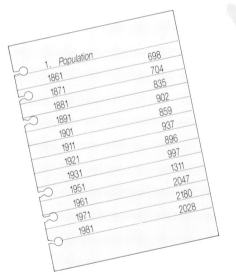

1. Population	
1861	698
1871	704
1881	835
1891	902
1901	859
1911	937
1921	896
1931	997
1951	1311
1961	2047
1971	2180
1981	2028

Figure 3

2. Age of residents (1981)	
0 – 4	3.2%
5 – 15	15.6%
16 – 24	14.5%
25 – 44	20.3%
45 – retired	26.5%
retired – 74	14.0%
75+	6.0%

VILLAGE SURVEY : DATA SHEET : SERVICES

Recorder _____

Date _____

Village _____

Local services	No. in Village
Service	
Baker	
Butcher	
Builder	
Church/Chapel	
Dairy/Milk Sales	
Doctor	
Garage	
Gen. Stores/Grocer	
Greengrocer	
Hairdresser	
Hardware	
Newsagent/ tobacconist	
Off Licence	
Police	
Post Office	
Post Box	
Pub	
Telephone	
Primary School	
Secondary School	
Village Hall	
Others (list)	

Mobile Services	Tick if available	No. of visits per week
Service		
Bread		
Butcher		
Doctor (part-time surgery)		
Fish		
Greengrocer		
Library		
Laundry		
Milk/Dairy		
Totals		

Public transport

Frequency   (per day/week)

Main Destination

Guidelines for the use of recording sheets

Record services provided rather than the presence of an establishment totally devoted to that service, eg. a post office with general store should be recorded as two services.

Figure 4

3 Figure 3 contains some statistics about Christleton obtained from census data in Chester library.

a Present the **population** information in the form of a line graph and the age structure in the form of a pie chart or a bar graph.

b Discuss as a class the possible reasons for the declines in population between 1891 and 1901, and 1911 and 1921.

c Why do you think there was a rapid increase between 1951 and 1961?

d Would you expect the population in 1991 to have stayed the same, increased or decreased, and why?

e To which age group do the greatest number of village residents belong?

f Would you say Christleton was an 'old' village or a 'young' village?

4 Carry out your own study of one or more local villages. To do this you should do the following:

● Carry out a survey of the village. To do this you will need a base map of the village to the scale of 1:10 000 and a survey sheet (see Figure 4). Walk around the village completing your survey sheet. Ask local people and look at noticeboards where you will often discover useful information. Take some photographs of the village. In walking around the village try to get a 'feel' for what it is like to live there. Do remember to be polite and courteous.

● Visit your local town library to find out more about the village. Go to the Reference Library and look at Census records to see how the population has changed. Look at 'The Domesday' computer disc completed in 1986 for further information.

DATA SHEET
OTHER ECONOMIC ACTIVITIES

Activity	No. in Village
Farms (within 2km)	
Agricultural Engineers	
Nursery/Market Gardens	
Haulier	
Others (list)	
	Total _____

Community activities
List activities:-

Tourist/visitor services

Service	No. in Village
Bed and Breakfast	
Cafe/Take-away	
Campsite	
Caravan site	
Field Centre/Outdoor Centre	
Gifts/Crafts	
Hotel/Guest House	
Holiday Flats/Chalets	
Restaurants	

Tax discs   Local   Non-local

VILLAGE SURVEY : DATA SHEET
– ENVIRONMENTAL INDEX –

Cosy	5 4 3 2 1	Bleak
Friendly	5 4 3 2 1	Unfriendly
Picturesque	5 4 3 2 1	Dull
Neat	5 4 3 2 1	Shabby
Colourful	5 4 3 2 1	Drab
Pleasant	5 4 3 2 1	Unpleasant
Quiet	5 4 3 2 1	Noisy
Unpolluted	5 4 3 2 1	Polluted
Well-maintained	5 4 3 2 1	Dilapidated
Historic	5 4 3 2 1	Modern
Varied	5 4 3 2 1	Uniform
Winding	5 4 3 2 1	Straight
Traffic Flow	5 4 3 2 1	Congested
Unspoilt	5 4 3 2 1	Commercialised

(Circle a number between 1–5 where 5 is "good" and 1 is "bad")

Total score _____

7.3   Studying Housing

House Types

There are many different types of house. There are **terraces**, **detached** houses and **flats** just to mention three. It is also possible to talk about houses in terms of their age – **Georgian**, **Victorian** and **inter-war** with each one having a particular style.

Activities

1 Look at Figure 1. It shows you some of the common types of house. In pairs try to think of a few more house types.

2 Make a simple sketch of the front of a house – it could be your own house. Try to identify the type of house and its approximate age using Figure 1 to help you. Add labels to your sketch.

3 Try to design a modern family detached house. You should make a labelled sketch to show the front of the house. If you wish, you could draw a **plan** to show the layout of the rooms within the house.

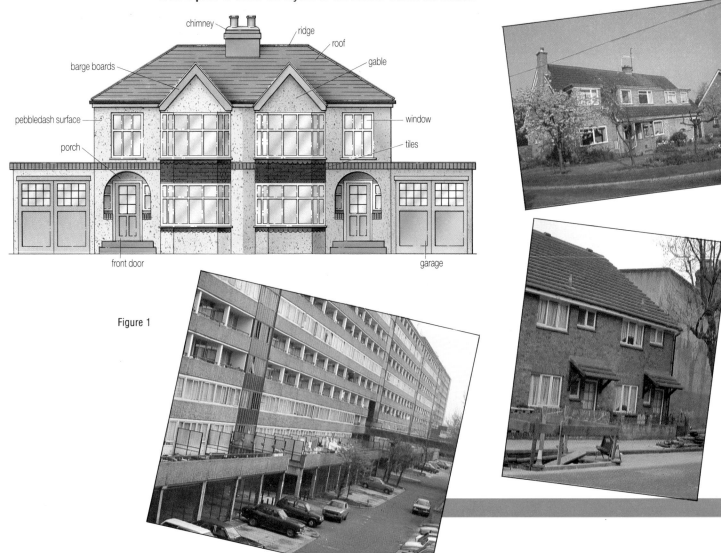

chimney
ridge
roof
gable
barge boards
pebbledash surface
porch
window
tiles
front door
garage

Figure 1

Housing Density

Density is a term used to describe the concentration of, for example people or houses, in an area. You have already come across **population density** in Chapter 6. In this section we will be studying **housing density**.

Houses in a town tend to be built closer together than in villages. This means that there is often a greater housing density in a town. Within a town, the greatest density tends to be in the centre where older and smaller houses are packed close together – this is the area where **terraced** housing (Figure 2) can be found. Further out from the centre, with more space for building, houses are bigger and less cramped. In these outer housing areas, called **suburbs** (Figure 3), most houses are **semi-detached** or **detached** and densities are lower.

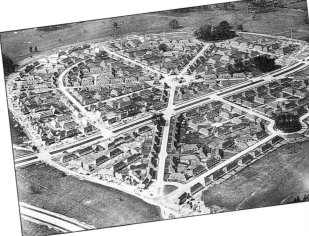
Figure 2 Terraced housing, Malton

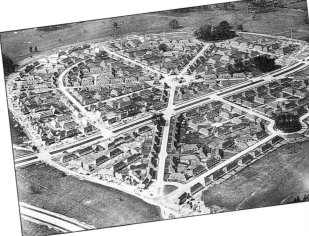
Figure 3 Early picture of Wembley, London Suburb

Activities

4 Figure 4 contains some extracts from a 1:2500 map. Notice how the outlines of houses and gardens can be seen quite clearly. Each house and garden occupies a **plot** of land.

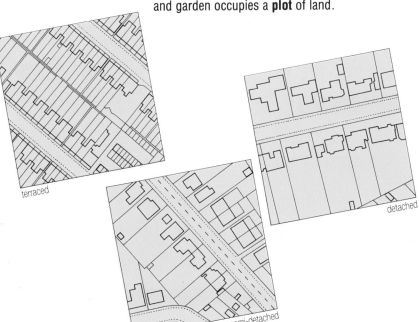
terraced

semi-detached

detached

Figure 4 Each square: 1 hectare

a Draw 3 sketches or make tracings to show the differences between the three types of house plot. Make sure that you draw them to approximately the same scale so that they can be compared. Identify the differences using labels, e.g. small front garden, shed, etc. Give each sketch a title. Figure 5 shows you what to do – it is a sketch of a **detached house plot**.

b Discover the housing densities for the three different house types. To do this count the number of houses (more than half a house counts as one) in each extract. Present your results in the form of a table – remember that your results will be 'per hectare'. Write a few sentences describing your results.

c Suggest where each type of house would probably be found in a town – near the centre or in the suburbs.

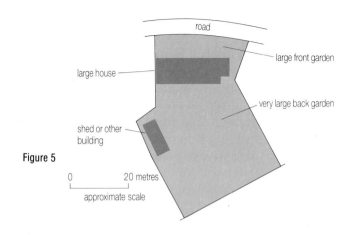

Figure 5

7.4   Shopping

Goods and services

When did you last go shopping and what did you buy? Some of you may have already been shopping today on your way to school when you probably bought sweets or something similar. When did you last buy clothes or a pair of shoes? Probably quite a while ago.

Sweets, clothes and shoes can all be thought of as **goods**. Going to the bank, the launderette or to the post office, to pay the TV licence, are examples of **services**.

We can divide goods and services into two kinds:

1 Those which are needed often and are usually cheap. For example, bread, sweets, newspapers. These are called **low order** or **convenience** goods and services.

2 Those which are needed less often and tend to be more expensive. Examples include electrical items, clothes and shoes. These are **high order** or **comparison** goods and services.

Shops can also be referred to as being low or high order, convenience or comparison.

Activities

1 Working in pairs, decide for each of the following whether they are high or low order.

a butcher	f vegetables
b chess set	g compact discs
c travel agent	h chemist
d newsagent	i cornflakes
e picture hooks	j hairdressers

2 Try to explain why the terms **convenience** and **comparison** are used for low and high order goods and services.

Studying the local shopping centre

Figure 1 is a sketch map of a local shopping centre. It probably contains the same sort of shops that your local centre has. What do you notice about the order of the shops? Are they mostly high or low order?

Figure 1

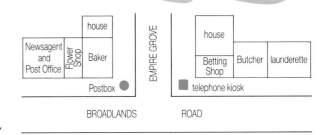

Activities

3 Make a sketch of your local shopping centre. Label each shop and state whether it is high or low order.

Figure 2

4 This Activity is best done in pairs and as a class so that results can be 'pooled'.
Study the **shopping patterns** at a local shopping centre.

a Make a copy of the **shopping questionnaire** (Figure 2). For a 20 minute period question as many people as you can. Be polite and explain that you are doing a survey as part of your Geography studies. Try to ask a range of people of differing ages.

Once back in the classroom, the results can be 'pooled' to form a **master table**. Make a copy of this as you will need it for the rest of the work.

b Show the information collected using the methods described in Figure 3. Describe and try to explain the results you have obtained. Are they as you expected?

c If possible, carry out a similar survey in your town centre. If this is not possible, you could ask your parents to tell you about their last visit to the town centre. Then 'pool' the results for the whole class.

Compare the results with those for the local centre. Are the goods bought high or low order? Are the shopping visits more or less often and what form of transport is most commonly used? Try to explain the trends and differences.

1. Goods shopped for
Groceries:
Greengrocers:
Chemist:
Bread (Baker):
Post Office:
Meat (Butcher):
Pet Supplies:
Electrical:
Clothes/shoes:
Records/tapes:
Fast Food:
D.I.Y.:
Furniture:
Newspapers/sweets:
Launderette:
Financial (Bank or Building Society):
Others:

2 Frequency of Visits
Daily:
2/3 times week:
Once a week:
2/3 times month:
Less often:

3. Mode of transport
Walk:
Car:
Bus:
Cycle:
Motorbike:
Lorry:
Train:

Use a tally system to record your results
e.g.   III = 3
       IIII = 5
       IIII III = 8 etc.

Figure 3

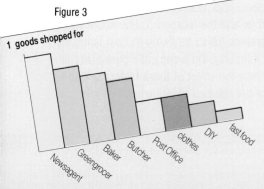

1 goods shopped for

2 frequency of visit

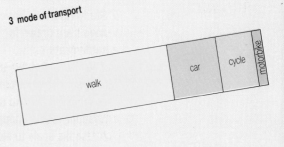

3 mode of transport

Spheres of Influence

Figure 4 shows **travel lines** and the **sphere of influence** for shoppers who visited the town of Great Missenden in Buckinghamshire. (Look ahead to Chapter 8 pages 62–72 to read about travel lines and spheres of influence.)

Generally speaking, people visiting their local shops do not travel very far so the sphere of influence is small. However, people visiting town centre shops for high order goods tend to travel further so forming a larger sphere of influence.

The shape of the sphere of influence is interesting as it is rarely a perfect 'sphere'. Uplands, rivers, alternative shopping centres and transport routes all affect the shape.

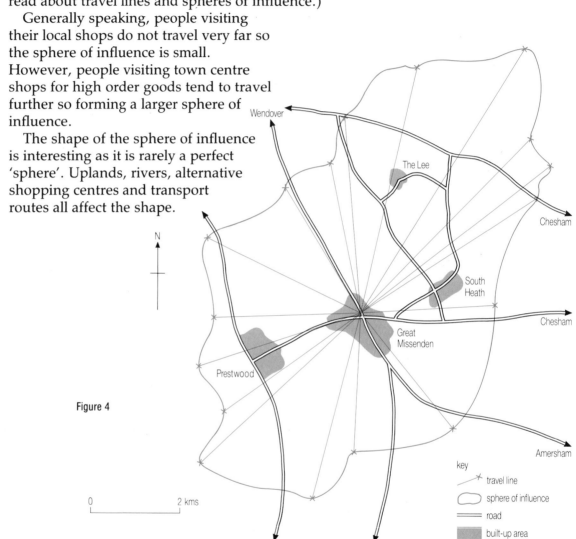

Figure 4

Activities

5 Study Figure 5. Notice that spheres of influence have been drawn for shoppers visiting two of the settlements.
 a Which of the two settlements has the largest sphere of influence?
 b Which of the two settlements is most likely supplying its shoppers with low order goods.
 c Use the scale to work out the maximum distance travelled by shoppers to the two centres.

d The shapes of the spheres on Figure 5 have been influenced by hills, roads, the coast, a river and the location of alternative shopping centres (other settlements competing for shoppers). On a copy of Figure 5 add labels to show the affect of these factors on the shapes of the spheres of influence.

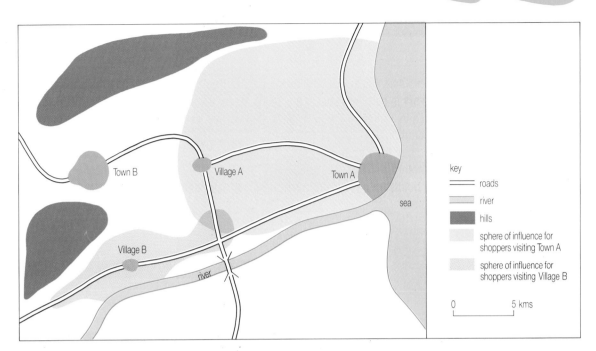

Figure 5

6 Carry out your own study of spheres of influence. You can do this for a local
shopping centre, a town centre or both. You need to ask about 30 people in
total where they have come from – make sure they have come to buy
something and are not just going to work! You will need a base map of the
area to plot their homes, the travel lines and the spheres of influence.
You could try to plot spheres for different goods and services, although this
is more difficult. In theory the higher the order, the larger the sphere – see if
this is true!

Modern shopping centres and hypermarkets

Most large towns have modern shopping
arcades. These often contain the large
chain stores found in most towns such as
Marks and Spencer and British Home
Stores. Nowadays some of these centres
are located on the edge of town close to
main roads or motorways (see Figure 6).

Hypermarkets are now becoming
common. These are huge shops
selling all sorts of items including
food, clothes, shoes, and garden
equipment under a single roof.

Figure 6 Brent Cross shopping centre

Activities

7 This Activity can take the form of a short quiz. Work in pairs to list as many chain stores as you can in 1 minute. Try to think of some of the less common ones. Score as follows: –
1 point for a correct chain store but which another pair has also listed
3 points for a chain store that no other pair has listed

8 Study the photograph in Figure 6.
a Try to explain why hypermarkets tend to locate on the edge of towns rather than in the centre.
b Use Figure 6 to suggest some important considerations when locating a hypermarket.
c Suggest a suitable site for a hypermarket near you. Study your local OS map and make a sketch map showing the site. Give reasons for your choice. Design an newspaper advert for your hypermarket.

7.5   Land uses in towns

There are many different types of land use in towns (see Figure 1). These include **housing**, **shops** and **offices**, **industrial** and **recreational**. Can you think of any others?

Each land use tends to group together to form a **zone**. Shops and offices tend to occur close together in the town centre – this zone is called the **Central Business District** (or CBD), industrial zones are often found along roads or canals. Houses aren't just dotted about all over the place – they tend to cluster together as **housing estates**.

It is interesting to study the location of the different land use zones in a town and to look for patterns. Figure 2 shows two simple patterns which can sometimes be seen to exist.

The oldest parts of a town are usually near the present day centre. Over the centuries towns spread outwards so that the newest parts are usually found on the outskirts. Sadly, many towns have had some of their old areas knocked down to make way for development. Does your home town fit this general pattern with the the oldest parts being near the centre and the youngest parts at the outskirts?

Figure 1

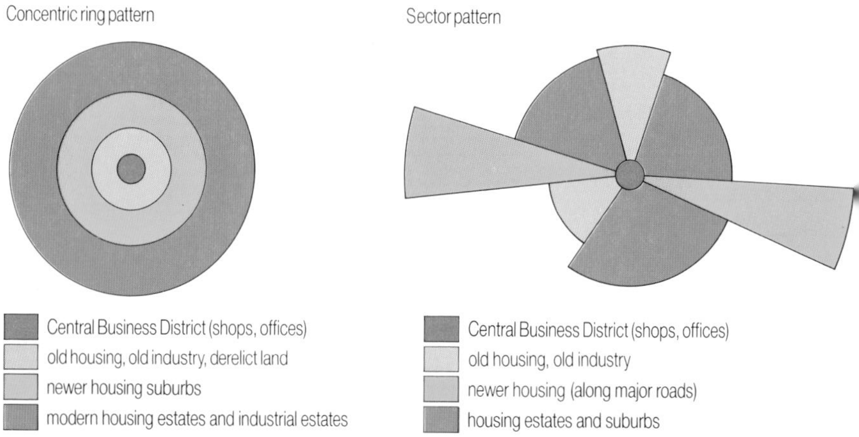

Concentric ring pattern

Sector pattern

Figure 2

Central Business District (shops, offices)
old housing, old industry, derelict land
newer housing suburbs
modern housing estates and industrial estates

Central Business District (shops, offices)
old housing, old industry
newer housing (along major roads)
housing estates and suburbs

A study of land uses in Malton, North Yorkshire

Malton is a small **market town** with a population of about 4 000 people. It nestles at the foot of the Wolds, a hilly area made of chalk, midway between York and Scarborough in the county of North Yorkshire (see Figure 3). Malton has a large influence over the surrounding farmlands. It has quite a wide range of shops and has two livestock markets (Figure 4) and one 'stalls' market every week. People travel many miles to attend the markets and the town becomes very congested on market days. The importance of markets to the town of Malton explains why we call it a market town.

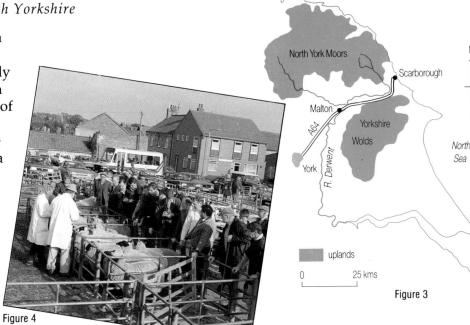
Figure 4

Figure 3

Activities

1 Figure 5 is a base map of Malton. It has been divided into grid squares. During a day's fieldwork a group of GCSE students recorded the main land use in each square. Their results are given in Figure 6.
Make a large copy of Figure 5 and complete a land use map of Malton. To do this give each land use in Figure 6 a different colour. Now use the information in Figure 6 to correctly locate and colour each grid square. Give your map a title and a key.

2 Having completed your map in Activity 1, answer the following questions:
   a Where does the CBD of Malton lie?
   b Which is the most important road through Malton? Why?
   c Where is Malton's industry concentrated? Is it possible to separate old and new industry? Explain your answer.
   d Can you pinpoint the old centre of the town? Does it coincide with the present position of the CBD?
   e Which land use takes up the most and which takes up the least area in the town?
   f Does Malton have any particular pattern of land use (see Figure 2)?

Figure 5

Figure 6

LAND USE CATEGORY	GRID SQUARE
Shops/office	G8, H8,I8, J8, I9, J9, J7, K9, K10,
Old Housing	I3, J4, J5, K5, K6, J6, I6, H6, G6, F6, E6 K7, I7, H7, G7, F7, L8, H9 – 13, G14, I10, J10, K11, L11, G11,
Newer Housing	B11, B12, B13, B14, C12, C13, C14, D12, D13, D14, E11, E12, E13, E14, F12, F13, G12, E5, F1–5, G1, G2, G3, G5, H1–5, I4, I5,
Industry	K12, K13, L9, L10, L12, L13, E9, E10, D9, D10, C9, C10, B9, B10,
Recreation/Open Space	F8, F9, F14, H14, I11, I12, I13, I14, J11, J12, J13, J14, K14, L14, L3, L4, L5, L6, L7, E1, E3, D2, D3, D4, D11, C11,
Transport	G9, G10, K8,
Cemetary	F10, F11,
Farmland	A1 – 14, B1 – 8, C1 – 8, D1, D5, D6, D7, D8, E7, E8, I1, I2, J1 – 3, K1 – 4, L1, L2,
Public Buildings	E2, E4, G4, G13,

7.6 The quality of our local environment

There are many factors which affect the quality of our lives. They include the amount of money we have, the size of our house, the amount of food we eat, and the amount of homework we get!

One important factor is the quality of our local environment. Most people agree that it is much more pleasant to live in an area where there are trees and flowers and where the streets are clean than to live in an area strewn with litter and next to a noisy motorway. In this unit you will be studying *your* local environment.

Activities

1 Look at the photographs in Figure 1.
  a Describe the scene in each photograph.
  b In which area would you prefer to live? Why?

2 Make a study of the **impact** of a building near you. It is most interesting to choose a large and relatively new building.

  Use the score sheet in Figure 2 to work out the impact of the building on the surrounding area to see how well it 'fits in'. It is best to work in pairs and for the whole class to study the same building. Scores could then be compared. You must remember that in this type of Activity there are no 'rights and wrongs'. Scores depend on personal views (people's perception).

  Repeat the Activity for several buildings.

Figure 1

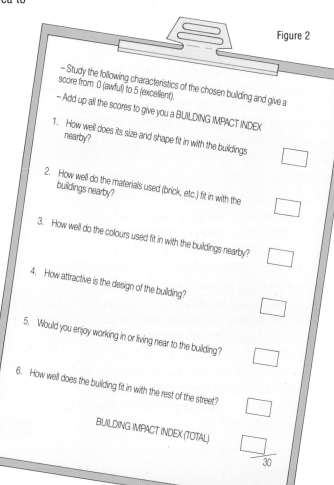

Figure 2

– Study the following characteristics of the chosen building and give a score from 0 (awful) to 5 (excellent).
– Add up all the scores to give you a BUILDING IMPACT INDEX

1. How well does its size and shape fit in with the buildings nearby?

2. How well do the materials used (brick, etc.) fit in with the buildings nearby?

3. How well do the colours used fit in with the buildings nearby?

4. How attractive is the design of the building?

5. Would you enjoy working in or living near to the building?

6. How well does the building fit in with the rest of the street?

BUILDING IMPACT INDEX (TOTAL)

30

3 Look at Figure 3. It gives a number of **environmental characteristics**. Notice how there are a number of opposites separated by numbers from 1–5. You have to score each characteristic with the highest score being the highest quality (to the right of the scoresheet). Scores can be indicated by drawing a ring around the chosen number. A total score can then be worked out.

a Make a study of your local environment. To do this you should make a copy of Figure 3 and survey your local area or street. You could also include photographs and sketches in your study – don't forget to label them! It would be useful to include a map too – remember you did one in Activity 1 page 3. How could your local environment could be improved – more trees or litter bins?

b Work in pairs to survey a larger area, for example, the streets around your school. Give each street a total score and draw a map to show the scores. Suggest reasons for the pattern of scores. Do the low scores relate to shopping areas or to main roads, for example? What could be done to improve the scores? done to improve the scores?

– SCORESHEET –

Draw a ring around the chosen number

1.	Boring	1	2	3	4	5	Interesting
2.	Artificial	1	2	3	4	5	Natural
3.	Dark	1	2	3	4	5	Light
4.	Dirty	1	2	3	4	5	Clean
5.	Enclosed	1	2	3	4	5	Open
6.	No trees	1	2	3	4	5	Lots of trees
7.	Noisy	1	2	3	4	5	Quiet
8.	Lots of parked cars	1	2	3	4	5	Few parked cars
9.	Broken pavement	1	2	3	4	5	Level pavement
10.	Smelly	1	2	3	4	5	Fresh
11.	Ugly	1	2	3	4	5	Attractive
12.	Poorly cared for houses and gardens	1	2	3	4	5	Well cared for houses and gardens

ENVIRONMENTAL INDEX (TOTAL) ☐ / 60

Figure 3

4 Discuss in small groups how the quality of environments can be improved. Are fines the answer to solving litter? Should more trees be planted? Suggest how the area around your school could be improved.

Dictionary

CBD Central Business District – a central area in towns containing mostly shops and offices.

comparison goods expensive goods bought infrequently, e.g. washing machine. Bought from comparison (**high order**) shops, e.g. department store.

convenience goods cheap goods required frequently, e.g. bread. Bought from convenience (**low order**) shops, e.g. bakers.

functions goods and services offered by a settlement (e.g. shops, recreation).

hypermarket huge shopping centre usually located on the edge of a large town.

market town a town which has had or still has important markets and is the economic focus of the surrounding area.

pedestrian precinct an area usually in the town centre where ordinary traffic is forbidden.

sphere of influence the area served by a town or function. The edge of this 'sphere' can be mapped as being the outer limit from where people will come.

suburbs housing estates built on the edge of towns. Most date back to 1930s or 1950s.

travel lines lines drawn on a map linking people's homes to functions, shops or town.

8 Transport

8.1 Journey to school

Figure 1 shows a group of children arriving at school. How many different forms of transport might they have used? Some of those walking may well have walked a short distance from a bus stop or a railway station.

Most of those people walking from home to school would probably live quite close to the school as walking is slow. Those who were dropped off by parents or perhaps travelled by train are likely to live further from school. In the following activities you will see how true these statements, or **hypotheses**, are.

Figure 1

Activities

1 a Each person in the class needs to find out the following information about their journey to school:
   - how far in kms do you travel from home to school?
   - how long does it take you to do the journey?
   - what is your main form of transport?

   b Use the information for the whole class to plot a **scattergraph** – see Figure 2. You should use a different symbol to show the different forms of transport.

   c When all the information has been plotted use a **best fit line** to show the trend of the points. Notice on Figure 2 how the best fit line has been drawn to roughly divide the points in half.

2 Use your graph to answer the following questions.

   a Look at Figure 3. It shows you how to understand a scattergraph. Is there a relationship between **distance travelled** and **time taken**? Is it positive or negative?

   b Look at Figure 2. Notice how, as journey time and distance increase, there is a change in the type of transport used. Is there a similar trend on your graph? Why do you think this is so?

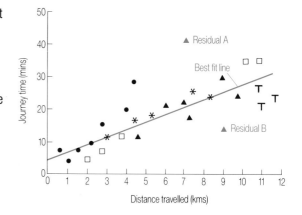

Key

- ● walk
- ▲ car
- ✳ bus
- ☐ bicycle
- **T** train

Figure 2

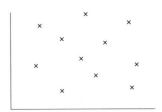

c On Figure 2 there are two points well away from the main trend. These are called **residuals**. There is often an interesting reason why they are there. Mark any residuals on your graph with a red ring. Now, as a class if you wish, suggest some **possible** reasons why these points do not fit in with the general trend. Ask the people concerned for the **real** reasons.

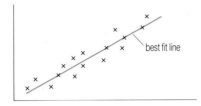

The points cluster together to show a trend – a **best fit line** can be drawn to make this clearer. This shows a good relationship between the two sets of information being plotted. In this graph there is a positive relationship (as one value increases, so does the other). A negative relationship (as one value increases, the other decreases) is shown in the graph below.

The points are all over the place! There is no clear trend. This shows NO relationship between the two sets of information being plotted.

Figure 3

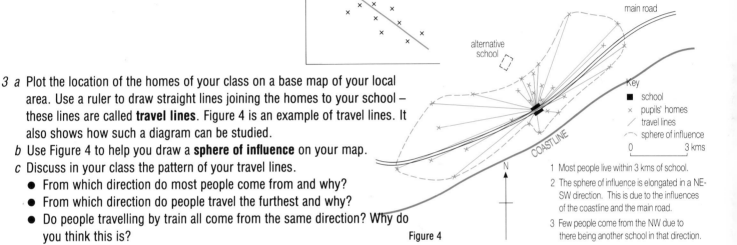

3 *a* Plot the location of the homes of your class on a base map of your local area. Use a ruler to draw straight lines joining the homes to your school – these lines are called **travel lines**. Figure 4 is an example of travel lines. It also shows how such a diagram can be studied.

b Use Figure 4 to help you draw a **sphere of influence** on your map.

c Discuss in your class the pattern of your travel lines.
- From which direction do most people come from and why?
- From which direction do people travel the furthest and why?
- Do people travelling by train all come from the same direction? Why do you think this is?

Key
- ■ school
- × pupils' homes
- / travel lines
- ⌒ sphere of influence
- 0 — 3 kms

1 Most people live within 3 kms of school.

2 The sphere of influence is elongated in a NE-SW direction. This is due to the influences of the coastline and the main road.

3 Few people come from the NW due to there being another school in that direction.

Figure 4

8.2 Measuring traffic flow

Figure 1

You may well have been in a traffic jam at some time in the last few days
Apart from being very annoying, traffic jams cause businesses to lose a great deal of money.

Many towns now have by-passes and **ring roads** to reduce the amount of traffic in the town centre and to relieve crowded (**congested**) roads.

Before plans are made to reduce traffic jams and congestion, **traffic flows** have to be studied. Figure 1 gives some of the questions a traffic planner would ask.

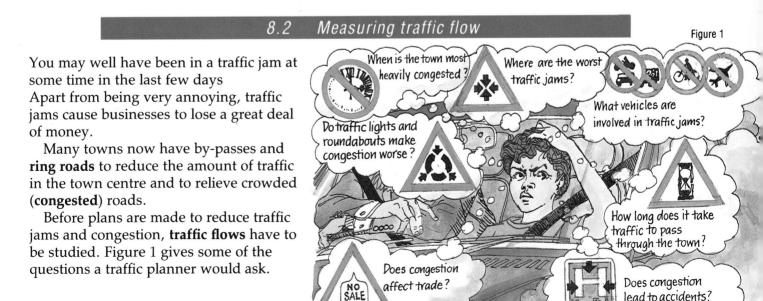

Activities

1 Carry out a traffic flow study in the roads around your school. To do this you should carry out the following steps taking care at all times to keep well away from the road unless, with your teacher, you have to cross it:

a Select an area where there are several roads and where some are busy and others less so. You might choose an area where there is much local debate about congestion or accidents.

b Divide into pairs. Each pair should then be given a particular stretch of road to observe (See Figure 2).

c At an agreed time start to count the traffic – one person calling out 'car . . . car . . . lorry . . . car . . .' etc and the other recording. Figure 3 shows you how to record the traffic. Record traffic travelling in **both** directions.

d After 10 minutes all groups should stop counting and return to the classroom. (Why do you think it is important that all groups do the count for exactly the same time period?)

e Results now need to be swapped so that everybody has the full set of results. Draw a master table.

Figure 2

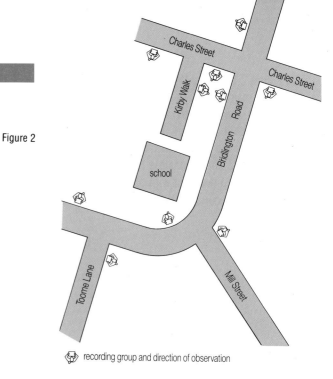

⬡ recording group and direction of observation

Figure 3

Recording sheet for traffic count						Names: _____ _____
Observation point: 4 Starting time: 10.00 a.m. Finishing time: 10.10 a.m.	Cars	Vans	Lorries	Buses	Bicycles	Total vehicles
	ℍℍ ℍℍ ℍℍ ⫼ (18)	ℍℍ ⎮ (6)	ℍℍ ℍℍ ⎮ (11)	⫼ (2)	⫼⎮ (3)	40

Figure 4

0   50   100 vehicles

f Using the **total vehicles** figures produce a **traffic flow map** (see Figure 4). You will need to work out a scale before you start. Your map should show the arrangement of the roads as they are in relation to the amount to traffic they have.

g Write up your study by including the following:
- a description of the way in which you collected the data. Were there any problems?
- a map of the roads studied by your class showing their layout and any features which influence traffic flow such as traffic lights or a roundabout
- a neat and carefully drawn traffic flow map
- a description of the map. Explain the patterns you observe. When would you expect there to be more traffic and when less?

2 If you wish, you could produce a more complex map where each flow line is divided into the different types of vehicle. A different colour could be used to show each type of vehicle. This will allow for a much more detailed discussion of patterns.

Although this may sound easy, it requires patience and great care!

You could also compare the traffic flowing in opposite directions by recording the two directions separately instead of combining them as in Activity 1.

3 Make a study, possibly as a wall display, of traffic flow issues. You could divide your display into **local** and **national** issues. Look for information about congestion, accidents due to congestion, planned by-passes, etc.

8.3   Car parking

There are many different places where cars can be parked. Figure 1 shows a few – can you think of any others? Towns and villages have **car parks** to try and prevent parking on the roadside which can cause traffic congestion and can block entrances. Generally speaking, the bigger the town, the more and larger the car parks.

Some car parks are free. Some are short term and others long term. How does the charging differ between short term and long term car parks? Some car parks are modern multi-storey parks whereas others make use of derelict land.

Figure 1

Activities

Activities 1 and 2 can be used to see whether there is a car parking problem in your town or village and whether or not a new car park needs to be built.

1 Plot the location of car parks on a base map of your local area. Locate the main shopping areas so that you can see how well placed the car parks are.

2 For one or more car parks do the following:

a Draw a sketch map to show the shape and layout of the car park. Locate entrances and exits, access to shops, facilities such as toilets and bottle banks, etc. Figure 2 is a sketch map of a town centre car park.

Figure 2

b Carry out a questionnaire (see Figure 3) of the car park users. You should aim to have a total of 30 questionnaires. Produce graphs to show the results (see page 55 to remind you how to draw bar graphs and pie charts). You could draw travel lines (see Figure 4 Unit 8.1) and a sphere of influence if you wish. Describe and suggest reasons for your results.

c At different times of day and on different days of the week count the number of vacant spaces in the car park. Also count the number of cars parked in improper places, i.e. not in the spaces marked out. Your results could be shown as a line graph (Figure 4). Comment on any patterns shown.

Figure 3

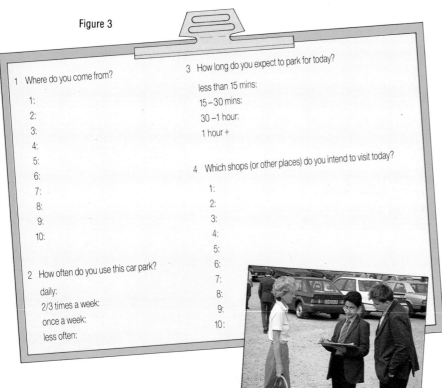

3 a Having carried out Activities 1 and 2, do you think your town or village needs a new car park? Explain your answer.

b If you think a new car park is needed suggest a possible site. Mark this on the map you drew in Activity 1 and write a few sentences giving the reasons for your choice.

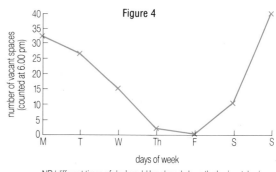

Figure 4

NB 'different times of day' could be placed along the horizontal axis

8.4   Choosing a by-pass route

Many towns and villages have a main road running through them. Nowadays, with so much traffic on the road, these towns often become heavily congested. This is because traffic wanting to pass through the town (**through traffic**) mixes with **local traffic** (shoppers, etc).

To relieve this congestion, by-passes have been built to divert through traffic away from the town centre.

Choosing a route for a by-pass is often very difficult and controversial. Farmers may lose valuable land, attractive woods may be felled and home owners may suddenly find a noisy road nearby. A lot of discussion needs to take place before a route is agreed and this may delay building for several years.

Activities

1 In this Activity your class has to choose a by-pass route for the town of Hartley. Figure 1 shows the area around Hartley and the two possible routes. Take time to study the routes closely.

There are two parts to this Activity.

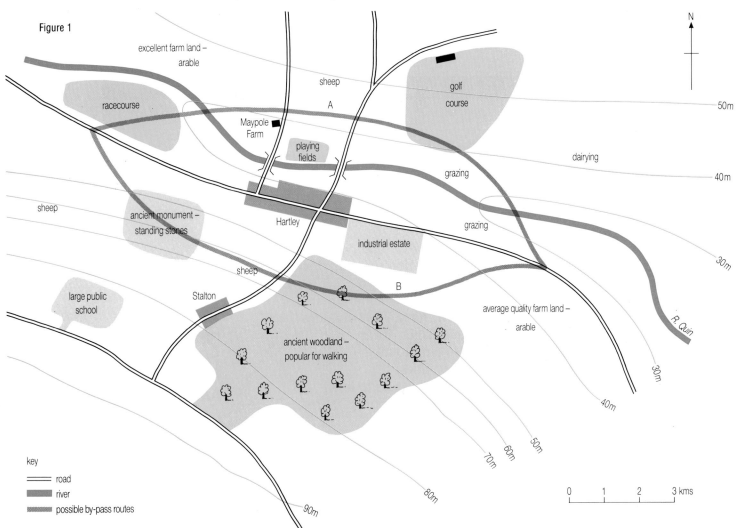

Figure 1

Part 1

The aim here is to examine the opinions of various people likely to be affected by the by-pass routes.

a To do this, the class needs to be divided into small groups. Each group should then take the part of one of the following people:

  ● Farmer at Maypole Farm who owns high quality arable farmland
  ● President of the golf club
  ● Chief Steward of the racecourse
  ● Local archaeologist
  ● Chairperson of Stalton Parish Council
  ● Representative of the National Trust which owns the ancient woodland
  ● Manager of a factory on the industrial estate

b The job of each group is to produce a small report suggesting the likely feelings of the person they represent to the proposed by-pass routes. Try to list reasons for their feelings.

c Each group should then report back to the whole class. Views can be discussed and rough notes taken of the opinions expressed.

Part 2

Now that you have a good idea of the strength of feeling of various people likely to be affected by the by-pass, you are in a much better position to try and decide upon a route.

a In **different** small groups or as individuals make two lists comparing the two routes:

  ● give reasons why Route A is better than Route B, and
  ● give reasons why Route B is better than Route A.

(There are several other considerations not yet mentioned – compare the length and therefore cost of the two routes; look at the relief of the land; how many road and river crossings need to be made; etc)

b Now decide on the best route and write a summary paragraph saying why you chose that route.

8.5   Networks and Accessibility

Networks

Look at Figure 1. It shows some of the main transport routes to the north of Chester (the map extract of Chester can be found on page 108).

Notice how the routes link together to form a **network**. As there are many roads in this area we can say that it has a **good** network.

Locate the A56 that links Chester with Helsby. Compare the route it takes with that of the railway. Notice that the road does not take a completely straight course between the two settlements as the railway does. Instead, it winds about linking together the small settlements in between. As the railway does not need to be connected to the smaller villages, it can take a straighter course. Motorways also tend to take a straighter course as they only link major cities.

Most roads are very old. Their early purpose was to link together villages to enable trading to occur. Transport was slow and few people travelled far from home. So, roads did not need to be built for long distance travel – instead they slowly grew to link places together.

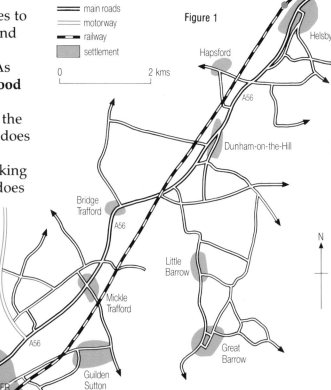

Figure 1

roads ('B' and minor)
main roads
motorway
railway
settlement

0   2 kms

Helsby
Hapsford
A56
Dunham-on-the-Hill
Bridge Trafford
A56
Little Barrow
Mickle Trafford
Great Barrow
A56
Guilden Sutton
CHESTER
N

Railways and motorways are more modern forms of transport. They carry freight and passengers over longer distances and between larger settlements. This is why they tend to have straighter courses than roads.

Activities

1 Draw a sketch map to show the course of the A56 and the railway between Chester and Helsby (see Figure 1). Mark on your map the small villages along the route of the A56.

2 There are many **physical** reasons why roads cannot take straight courses. Make a list of some of the possible reasons.

3 Try to discover why some of the oldest roads in Britain, **Roman roads**, were so straight in comparison with the roads that developed later.

Accessibility

If a place can be reached easily from other places, it is said to be very **accessible**. If a place is difficult to get to, it is **inaccessible**.

Accessibility is important especially for business. Shopowners, for example, want their shops to be easily accessible for their customers. This is why there are few shops in remote parts of the country.

Accessibility can be measured using the **Shimbel Index**. This is described in Figure 2.

Figure 2

1 Produce a simplified map showing the routes between places (A-E).

Key
● Nodes – places or junctions
— Arcs – links between nodes

2 Produce a table to discover the minimum number of arcs between places

		TO				
	A	B	C	D	E	TOTAL
A	-	2	4	3	3	12
B	2	-	2	2	2	8
C	4	2	-	2	4	12
D	3	2	2	-	2	9
E	3	2	4	2	-	11

FROM

3 The TOTAL figure is the SHIMBEL INDEX. The lowest figure is the most accessible and the highest figure is the least accessible. In this example B is the most accessible and A and C the least accessible.

Activities

4 Figure 3 is a simplified map of the main road network to the north of Chester. Discover the most accessible settlement by working out the Shimbel Index. Follow the steps in Figure 2.

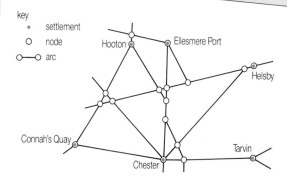

key
● settlement
○ node
○—○ arc

Figure 3

8.6   Map Study of Chester

The following activities relate to the map extract of Chester on page 108.

Activities

1 What is the motorway that runs northwards from the east of Chester?

2 a Identify the A41(T) (which becomes the A55 (T)) that runs around the east and south sides of Chester. What name is given to such a road running around the outskirts of a town?
  b What is the purpose of such a road?
  c What does the (T) stand for?
  d Is it single or dual carriageway?
  e You have travelled from the junction of the A56 and the motorway (432687) to the junction of the A483 and A55 (T) (390625) using the A41(T) and the A55(T). How many kilometres have you travelled?

3 What evidence is there to suggest that Chester may have been an important town during Roman times?

4 You are the new warden of the Chester youth hostel (397651) and you need to produce a simple map to show people how to get there.
In rough first, and then neatly, draw a sketch map to show people how to reach the hostel from the main bus station in the centre of Chester. Your map should be accurate and clear. Show landmarks and give written directions to help. Use road numbers if possible.

8.7   Major transport routes in Britain

Figure 1 shows the motorways, main roads and railways in Britain. Notice how the pattern or **network** is most dense in central and southern Britain. This is because there is a great demand from passengers and industry. Further north and west, there are fewer people and fewer industries to serve.

Most of the main roads and railways radiate out of London, the capital. Some of the roads, for example the A5, are very ancient and date back to Roman times. Such roads tend to have long straight stretches – do you have any near you? The motorways are most dense around the major cities such as London, Birmingham and Manchester. Motorway building is very expensive (over £1 million a kilometre!) so they are only built where there is great demand.

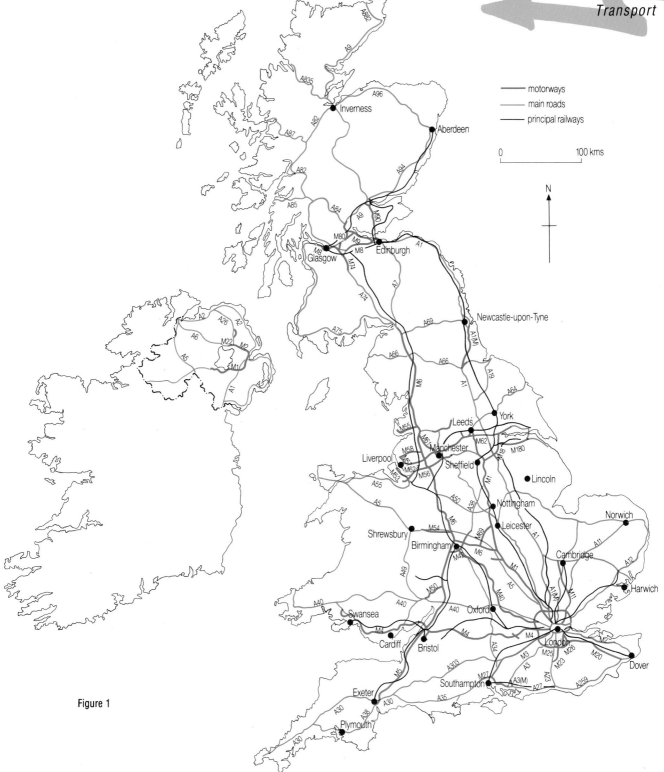

Figure 1

Activities

1 Along what motorways/roads would you travel between the following places –
   a Birmingham and Shrewsbury
   b Aberdeen and Inverness
   c Oxford and Manchester

2 Which major cities are found at either end of the following motorways?
   a M1
   b M5
   c M3

Figure 2

Distance in miles ← | Distance chart | → Distance in kilometres

Distances in kilometres (upper-right of chart, from each city across):

LONDON	810 169 196 87 253 114 608 277 639 122 863 304 156 211 325 298 441 183 196 92 351 256 241 124 312 311
ABERDEEN	676 793 737 789 927 201 916 233 813 169 526 666 616 549 547 378 764 610 777 990 579 642 880 795 513
BIRMINGHAM	130 161 166 283 470 253 470 269 737 182 63 145 150 129 333 267 80 103 327 122 72 206 192 209
BRISTOL	232 72 299 600 122 600 307 867 312 193 275 259 259 463 356 233 119 196 259 166 122 137 340
CAMBRIDGE	288 201 539 354 58 108 793 233 109 137 270 243 370 100 134 134 423 193 233 211 349 241
CARDIFF	383 620 195 620 396 884 354 229 311 272 277 489 388 246 174 269 288 179 195 66 393
DOVER	723 399 753 201 977 418 270 325 439 412 555 280 311 206 465 370 356 230 441 425
EDINBURGH	724 71 665 254 325 455 415 348 346 177 589 422 575 798 78 441 678 631 312
EXETER	723 399 995 435 315 389 381 380 586 454 356 229 74 81 288 169 259 462
GLASGOW	695 267 346 486 446 348 346 238 620 446 573 797 399 438 676 594 349
HARWICH	877 359 217 249 378 385 496 117 241 203 473 301 354 246 430 367
INVERNESS	579 742 687 615 600 431 801 692 829 1069 632 705 932 861 566
LEEDS	153 109 121 64 148 283 113 270 509 53 175 33 365 39
LEICESTER	82 161 148 301 192 40 117 389 100 135 220 254 174
LINCOLN	190 135 256 169 56 200 472 74 188 303 336 121
LIVERPOOL	56 249 354 158 253 455 116 93 356 146 159
MANCHESTER	212 298 101 232 455 61 111 335 301 103
NEWCASTLE-UPON-TYNE	425 253 418 660 201 323 521 513 135
NORWICH	196 233 552 235 330 311 441 291
NOTTINGHAM	158 430 60 132 261 272 124
OXFORD	298 217 171 103 227 291
PLYMOUTH	455 362 243 332 536
SHEFFIELD	132 320 322 84
SHREWSBURY	274 190 214
SOUTHAMPTON	602 357
SWANSEA	404

Distances in miles (lower-left of chart, from each city across):

ABERDEEN	503
BIRMINGHAM	105 420
BRISTOL	122 493 81
CAMBRIDGE	54 458 100 144
CARDIFF	157 490 103 45 179
DOVER	71 576 176 186 125 238
EDINBURGH	378 125 292 373 335 385 449
EXETER	172 569 157 76 220 121 248 450
GLASGOW	397 145 292 373 360 385 468 44 449
HARWICH	76 505 167 191 67 246 125 413 248 432
INVERNESS	536 105 458 539 493 549 607 158 618 166 545
LEEDS	189 327 113 194 145 220 260 202 270 215 223 360
LEICESTER	97 414 39 120 68 142 168 283 196 302 135 461 95
LINCOLN	131 383 90 171 85 193 202 258 247 277 155 427 68 51
LIVERPOOL	202 341 93 161 168 169 273 216 237 216 235 382 75 100 118
MANCHESTER	185 340 80 161 151 172 256 215 236 215 239 373 40 92 84 35
NEWCASTLE-UPON-TYNE	274 235 207 288 230 304 345 110 364 148 308 268 92 187 159 155 132
NORWICH	114 475 166 221 62 241 174 366 282 385 73 498 176 119 105 220 185 264
NOTTINGHAM	122 379 50 145 83 153 193 262 221 277 150 430 70 25 35 98 63 157 122
OXFORD	57 483 64 74 83 108 128 357 142 356 126 515 168 73 124 157 144 260 145 98
PLYMOUTH	218 615 203 122 263 167 289 496 46 495 294 664 316 242 293 283 283 410 343 267 185
SHEFFIELD	159 360 76 161 120 179 230 235 237 248 187 393 33 62 46 72 38 125 146 37 135 283
SHREWSBURY	150 399 45 103 145 111 221 274 179 272 220 438 109 84 117 58 69 201 205 82 106 225 82
SOUTHAMPTON	77 547 128 76 131 121 143 421 105 420 153 579 232 137 188 221 208 324 193 162 64 151 199 170
SWANSEA	194 494 119 85 217 41 274 392 161 369 267 535 227 158 209 153 187 319 274 169 141 206 200 118 161
YORK	193 319 130 211 150 244 264 194 287 217 228 352 24 108 75 99 64 84 181 77 181 333 52 133 245 251

Figure 2

3 Your family is planning to visit several relatives and you have been asked to plan a route. You live in Exeter and have relatives in Oxford, Sheffield, Southampton, Bristol and Shrewsbury.

Suggest a round trip starting and finishing at Exeter. Describe the route between the towns giving the road/motorway numbers. Use the **distance chart** (Figure 2) to suggest the distances between each of the places. What is the total distance that you will have covered?

4 Use an atlas to suggest why there are no major railways in central Wales.

Dictionary

accessibility how easy it is to reach a place.

by-pass/ring road a road that keeps traffic out of town centres. It often forms a 'ring' around a town.

congestion overcrowding of cars or people.

network a number of transport routes linked together.

Shimbel Index a measure of accessibility

sphere of influence the area served by, for example, a school or a shop.

travel lines straight lines drawn on a map showing the movement of people between two places, e.g. home and school.

9 Farming

Whilst eating a packet of crisps during break, it is hard to imagine that the crisps started life as dirty potatoes growing within the soil probably in eastern England. Almost all the processed food that we eat comes from a **raw** source of vegetable or animal product.

If you examine the labels of foods you can see the list of ingredients. They are given in order by weight – it is interesting to note that **sugar** often appears as the first on the list and we all know that too much sugar is harmful to our health!

Also on the labels is **dietary** or **nutritional** information. This is usually split into **proteins, carbohydrates, fats, fibre**, and **additional additives**. It is interesting to see how much of each substance common foods contain.

Figure 1 gives some examples of ingredients and nutritional information for some common foods. As you can see, most of the ingredients are home produced by farmers in Britain.

Food	Ingredients	Nutritional Information (amount per 100 grams)					Source of ingredients
		Prot.	Carb.	Fats	Fibre	Add Addit.	
Pickle	Vinegar, sugar, cauliflower, swedes, onions, apples, flour, treacle, salt, sultanas, spices	0.5	31.1	–	1.1	–	All from UK except: spices from Nigeria, USA, W. Indies, India; sultanas from Australia, Greece, Turkey.
Twiglets	Wholemeal flour, veg. fat, yeast extract, salt, cheese, wheat starch, pepper.	11.9	60.2	12.9	incl. in carb.	–	UK except: oil from Malaysia and USA; cheese from Denmark; pepper from Indonesia.
Baked beans	Beans, water, tomato purée, sugar, salt, maize starch, spices	5.5	14.1	0.5	5.4	–	Beans from USA; tomato purée from Southern Europe; maize starch from USA; spices from Egypt, Italy, Indonesia, W. Africa Jamaica, Mexico.

Most of the ingredients are produced in Britain – the vegetables, flour, some of the fruit and probably some of the sugar. The spices, sultanas and beans will have been imported from abroad.

Figure 1

Activities

1 Use your Science textbook to discover more about the various food substances listed above. Try to identify the importance of each substance to our health and diet. List some foods which are high in each substance. Why is it important to have a **balanced diet**?

2 a Draw three **proportional bars** to show the nutritional information in Figure 1 for pickle, twiglets and baked beans. Draw each bar 10 cms high – this represents 100 grams, so 1 cm = 10 grams. Make each bar 2 cms wide. Use a different colour for each food substance and shade each bar accordingly.
b Which food provides the most carbohydrates?
c Which food provides the most fibre?
d Try to explain why part of each of your bars is left uncoloured.

3 Make a study of ingredients and nutritional information of some common breakfast foods. List the different ingredients and nutritional information (where available) and suggest whether they came from Britain or abroad.

Information could be collated for the whole class and a display made of labels and packets showing the different breakfast food products eaten by your class.

9.2 The Farming System

Look at Figure 1. It shows how a farm can be thought of as a **system**. There are **inputs** into the system such as labour and seeds, **farm processes** such as milking cattle and **outputs** such as eggs or potatoes. A systems diagram like Figure 1 helps us to understand the workings of a farm.

All farmers have to decide what to do with their land. Some farmers use computers to help them decide whilst others use their own judgement perhaps continuing to farm as they have done for many years. Each farmer will consider the various factors in the farm system. The way a farmer views the factors is his/her **perception**. In Britain, farmers are concerned with making a profit – they are **commercial** farmers.

Figure 1

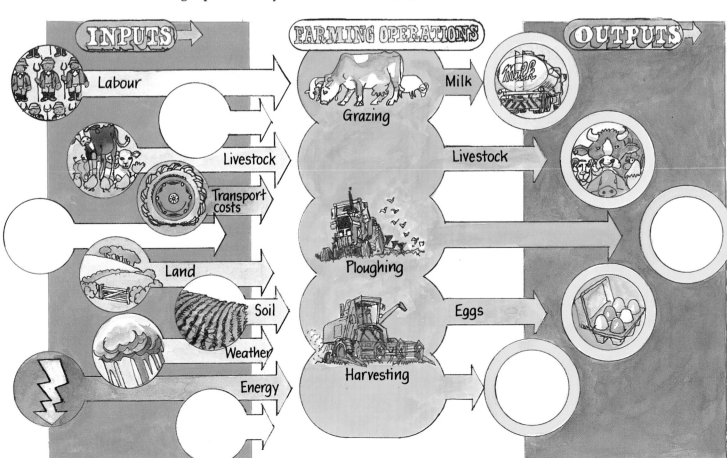

Activities

1 Figure 2 contains some aspects of the **farm system** which are not in Figure 1. Make a copy of Figure 1 adding the aspects in Figure 2 in their correct places.

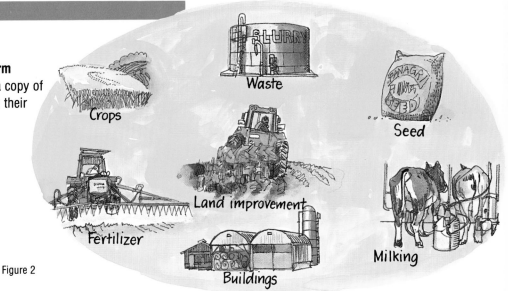

Figure 2

9.3   Farm Case Studies

Some of you may live on a farm. Some of you may live close to a farm or have friends of your family who are farmers. However, many of you will never have been on a farm at all. The two detailed farm studies in this chapter will help you understand a little of what farming is all about.

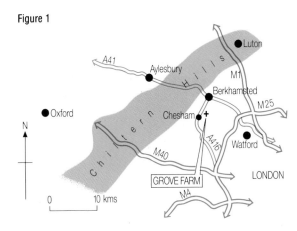

Figure 1

Grove Farm, Chesham, Buckinghamshire.

Figure 1 shows the location of Grove Farm. It is roughly halfway between Chesham and Berkhamsted some 30 kms NW of London. The farm is owned by Mr Harman – it has been in his family since 1919.

Figure 2 shows the layout of Grove Farm. The photographs (Figures 3 & 4) show you what his land is like. Notice how the soil has a white tinge to it – this is **chalk** as Grove Farm is on part of the Chiltern Hills which are made of chalk.

Figure 2

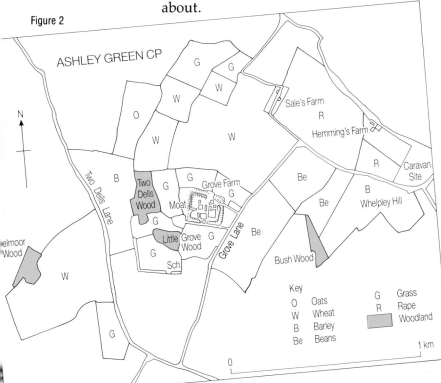

Key
O   Oats
W   Wheat
B   Barley
Be   Beans
G   Grass
R   Rape
Woodland

1 km

In the Chesham area, there is a thin covering of clay which makes the soil quite fertile. Chalk is a **permeable** rock which means that is lets water pass through it. Mr Harman's land is well drained.

Most of Mr Harman's land is ploughed and used for growing cereals (**arable**). He concentrates mainly on **wheat** which is used for making flour. He also grows some **barley** (for cattle feed and malt) and **oats** (cattle feed). The wheat and malting barley are marketed in Newmarket. The cattle feed is used on the farm.

Mr Harman cannot grow the same crop in a field year after year because the soil would soon become infertile and the production (**yield**) would decline. Also, disease might spread through his crop. Like most arable farmers, Mr Harman has a **rotation** system where every third year a different crop is grown to add nutrients to the soil. Such a crop is called a **break** crop. Mr Harman uses two break crops:

Figure 3

Figure 4

Figure 5

- **oilseed rape** – the yellow crop that many of you will be familiar with is grown to produce oil for margarine. It is also sent to Newmarket.
- **beans** – these add important nutrients to the soil. Mr Harman sells his beans to be exported to West Germany as cattle feed.

Mr Harman also keeps 100 high quality Charolais cattle, the white cattle in Figure 5. These are bred and sold to private breeders in Perth, Scotland. The poorer quality animals go to market in Banbury.

The labour force on Grove Farm is small. Apart from Mr Harman and his son, there are two men on the arable side and one livestockman. A young man is employed as part of a government training scheme. There is a great deal of machinery, which is why such a small labour force is needed, including three tractors – a new tractor cost £30 000 in 1989 -, ploughs, drills and cultivators. He does not own his own combine harvester – this work is done by an outside contractor.

Grove Farm contains some areas of woodland (see Figure 2). Mr Harman has looked after these areas very carefully as he feels that it is important that farmers look after the countryside by providing natural habitats for birds, animals and plants.

Activities

1 a What is **crop rotation** and why do farmers like Mr Harman operate such a system?

b Oilseed rape can be harvested using combine harvesters. How does this fact help to explain why so many cereal farmers like to grow oilseed rape as a break crop?

c What is the main reason for growing beans as a break crop?

2 a Produce a bar chart or pie graph to show the hectares of crops grown on Grove Farm in 1989.

crop	hectares
oilseed rape	48
beans	32
barley	30
wheat	135
oats	5
grass (for grazing)	50

b What is the total hectarage farmed?

c What is the largest hectarage used for?

d What is this crop used to produce?

(1 hectare is approximately the size of a football pitch)

3 Use an atlas to help you with this Activity. Make a large neat copy of the map shown in Figure 1. Use arrows to show the destination (**market**) of the products from Grove Farm.

To do this you need to first locate the farm in your atlas. Now look up the location of Banbury where some of the cattle are sold. Use a ruler to draw an arrow in pencil on your map from Grove Farm pointing in the gereral direction of Banbury. Write **Banbury** at the end of your arrow. Now go over your arrow with a colour to represent **cattle** – explain this in a key.
Now continue for the other farm products using different colours for the different products. Use the text to find out where the markets are.
Title your map 'The markets for the products of Grove Farm'.

4 Study Figure 2 showing the layout of Grove Farm.

a How many fields are used for growing barley?

b How do the size of the fields used for wheat compare to those used for grass? Try to explain your observations.

c Most of the cattle grazing is done on the fields closest to the farm buildings. Why do you think this is so?

d Name the woods on Mr Harman's land.

Figure 6

5 Figure 6 shows the main building on Grove Farm. It is a general purpose building. Describe what it is being used for.

6 This is a discussion Activity. You will need to work in pairs or small groups. One person in each group should keep a written record of what is said. A whole-class discussion could then take place with each group reporting its thoughts. Discussions could be tape recorded.

a Some modern farmers have removed hedges and woodland in order to create bigger and bigger fields.

- why do you think they have done this?
- how might this affect wildlife?
- should farmers be allowed to remove hedges and woodland?

b Many farms are criss-crossed by public footpaths (see the photograph in Figure 4). You have probably walked some such paths.

- why might some farmers be unhappy about these footpaths crossing their land?
- why is it in the farmer's best interest to keep paths well maintained and clearly signposted?

Activities

Barton farm

Liverpool

M56

A56

Chester

A51

Cheshire
Plain

Barton Farm

Cambrian

Wrexham

A534

A41

A483

M6

Stoke
on Trent

Whitchurch

Mountains

N

0   20 kms

Barton Farm, Cheshire : a pastoral farm (grazing livestock on grass)

Hectarage: 66   Labour: farmer (Mr Humphreys) and son

Buildings: cubicle buildings for cows, silage pit, modern sheds for young cattle, milking parlour.

Machinery: 3 tractors, plough, cultivator, baler, hedge cutter, sprayer.

Crops: barley (11 hectares) to feed cattle. None sold. Rest of farm grass.

Livestock: dairy cows (60) milked twice a day, replacement young stock (36), beef cattle (20).

Physical factors affecting land use: the climate is wet and mild – this is ideal for grass growing and animal grazing. The soils are mainly clay. This means that they are cold and wet – also ideal for grass but poor for cereals. The landscape is gently rolling.

Most profitable enterprise: milk, collected by the Milk Marketing Board in refrigerated lorries and taken to the dairy at Stretton (2 kilometres due south of Barton Farm); some surplus cattle sold by auction at Beeston.

Irrigation: none.

Fertilisers: nitrogen applied to barley and grass, phosphorous and potash to barley.

Pesticides: sprayed when necessary.

Effect of the EC: milk quotas restrict the amount of milk that can be produced on each farm. Barton Farm has started to keep beef cattle in order to retain profits.

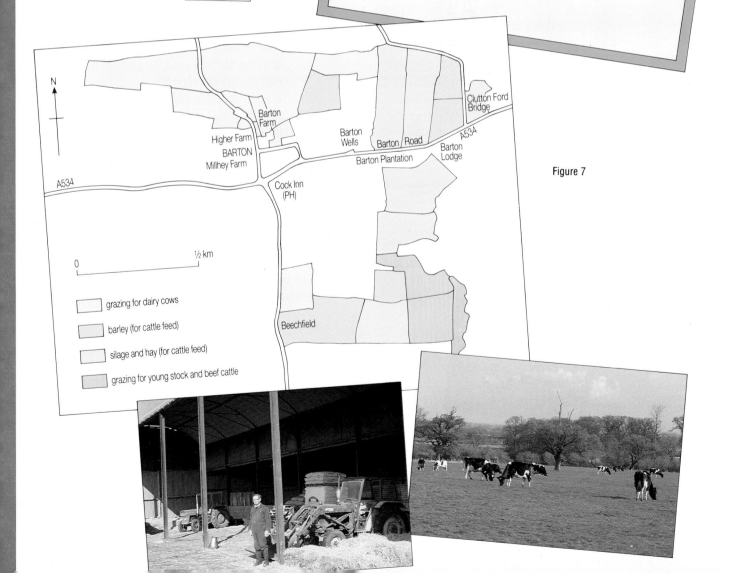

N

Clutton Ford
Bridge

Barton
Farm

Barton
Wells

Barton   Road

A534

Higher Farm

BARTON
Millhey Farm

Barton Plantation

Barton
Lodge

A534

Cock Inn
(PH)

Beechfield

0   ½ km

☐ grazing for dairy cows

☐ barley (for cattle feed)

☐ silage and hay (for cattle feed)

☐ grazing for young stock and beef cattle

Figure 7

1 For this Activity you will need a sheet of tracing paper.
   a Lay your tracing paper over the aerial photograph Figure 8. With reference to the land use map in Figure 7, use a pencil first and then colours if you wish to mark on the following:

   - main roads including the 'square' at Barton,
   - the rough extent of Barton village,
   - Barton Farm,
   - the fields belonging to Mr Humphreys
   - Barton plantation and the other unnamed wood to the south of the map
   - north point
   - scale

   b Use different colours to shade the different land uses on your map. Figure 7 describes what each field was used for in 1989.
   c Give your map a title.

2 Use your map completed in Activity 1, and Figures 7 and 8 to answer the following questions.
   a How many fields belong to Barton Farm?
   b Use the scale to work out the approximate size of the smallest and the largest fields.
   c What are the fields closest to the farm mainly used for? Try to explain your answer.

   d What are the fields furthest from the farm mainly used for? Try to explain your answer.
   e How many fields are used to grow barley?
   f Look carefully at Figure 8. Look at the fields where barley was grown in 1989. What evidence is there to suggest that barley may not have been grown in these fields when the photograph was taken in 1985?

3 Produce a **farm system** diagram for Barton Farm showing the inputs, the farm processes and the outputs.

4 a What is the main enterprise on Barton Farm? How does this compare to the main enterprise on Grove Farm?
   b What are the physical reasons why Mr Humpreys concentrates on livestock at Barton Farm?
   c Why does Mr Humphreys grow some barley?
   d Why has Mr Humphreys recently started to fatten beef cattle?

5 Discuss with your neighbour the main differences between the two farms – the arable **Grove farm** and the pastoral **Barton farm**. Try to list 10 differences using the maps and text.

Figure 8

The Hereford farm game

Mr Evans owns Bridge Farm which is located just outside the town of Hereford in the county of Hereford and Worcester. He is going abroad for three years and you have been asked to run his farm while he is away.

Your job is to decide which crops to grow in the 'free choice' fields. Your aim is to make as big a profit as possible. Study the information in Figure 1. It shows the layout of the fields, their size and the crops to be grown. Although you will have to choose what to grow in most fields (the 'free choice' fields), notice that there is no choice in the others.

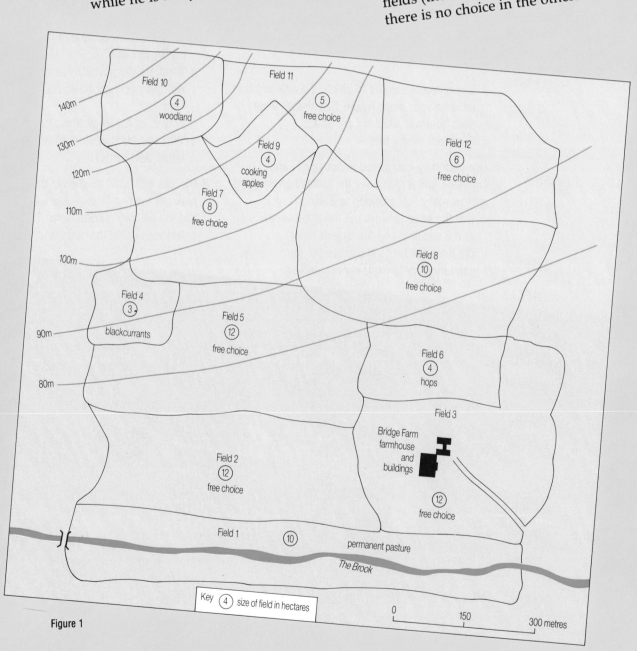

Figure 1

Key ④ size of field in hectares

Playing the game

1 Make a copy of the map Figure 1. On this you will show what is grown in Year 1 – Mr Evans has asked you to do this. Make up your own symbols to show the crops which must continue to be grown in the non-'free choice' fields. Explain your symbols in a key.

2 Now decide which crops to grow in the seven 'free choice' fields. You have to have two fields of **sugar beet** but no more as you are under contract from the British Sugar Corporation. Apart from those two fields you can grow what you like from the following list:

- **wheat**
- **barley**
- **peas**

To decide what to grow you need to study the Profit Table (Figure 2). This tells you the profit of each crop per hectare.

Notice that the profit changes with different weather conditions. Your teacher will shake dice to find the weather - notice that 'wet and warm' and 'wet and cool' are more likely to occur than 'dry and warm' and 'dry and cool'. You should bear this in mind when making your choices. Also, remember that the fields are different sizes.

3 Make a copy of the **account sheet** (Figure 3) and record your choices for Year 1 in the correct spaces.

4 Use symbols to show your choice of crops on your map of the farm. Add these symbols to the key.

5 Your teacher will now shake the dice to find out the weather.

6 Once the weather is known, you can work out your profit for the year by multiplying the profit per hectare by the number of hectares in the field.

e.g. say you decided to grow peas in field 8 and it was a 'warm and wet' year. Your profit would be:

£125 (profit per hectare when the weather is 'warm and wet') × 10 (number of hectares in field 8) = £1250.

Write your profits for each field including those where you did not have a choice on the Account Sheet.

7 Work out your **total profit** for Year 1.

8 Compare your profit with others in your class.

9 Don't forget to complete your map (Activity 1) to show Mr Evans what you grew in year 1.

Figure 3

Field No.	Year 1 Crops	Income (£)	Year 2 Crops	Income (£)	Year 3 Crops	Income (£)
1	pasture					
2			pasture			
3					pasture	
4	blackcurrants					
5			blackcurrants			
6	hops				blackcurrants	
7			hops		hops	
8						
9	cooking apples		cooking apples			
10	woodland				cooking apples	
11			woodland		woodland	
12						
Total						

Total incomes each year	
Year 1	total income
Year 2	total income
Year 3	total income
GRAND TOTAL	

Figure 2

Profits for various crops and land uses (in £ per hectare)

	WET WARM (Dice 1 or 2)	WET COOL (Dice 3 or 4)	DRY WARM (Dice 5)	DRY COOL (Dice 6)
pasture (dairy cows)	250	250	125	60
blackcurrants	150	75	250	100
cooking apples	305	205	305	80
hops	360	270	445	270
barley	50	50	65	65
wheat	40	30	85	65
peas	125	15	45	30
sugar beet	120	40	65	15
oats	60	40	85	25
beans	115	40	55	40
woodland	0	0	0	0

10 Continue in the same way for Years 2 and 3 and work out your **grand total** profit for the 3 years.

Having played the game, try to answer the following questions:

1 Why do you think you are not allowed to change the fields containing:
   a pasture
   b fruit and hops
   c woodland?

2 What are hops used for?

3 Why do you think the profit for woodland is £0?

4 Why do you think field 10 is used for woodland?

5 Why do you think field 1 is used for pasture with dairy cows?

6 Why does the profit of a crop depend on the weather?

7 Why would it not be very sensible to grow the same crop in every field year after year. There are two main reasons – see if you can think of them both!

To play a more advanced version of the game you should work in pairs or in small groups. Include **oats** and **beans** in your range of choices for the 7 'free choice' fields.

Also, add further restrictions to the maximum and minimum number of fields that can be used for each crop (Figure 4).

Play the game for 5 years rather than 3.

Having played the more advanced version, discuss the following questions:

8 How true to life do you think the farm game is?

9 How could the game be made even more true to life?

Figure 4

	Maximum	Minimum
Barley	2	0
Wheat	2	0
Peas	3	1
Sugarbeet	2	2
Oats	2	1
Beans	3	1

Dictionary

arable land under the plough.
break crop a crop such as oilseed rape or beans which forms a 'break' in a succession of the same crop being grown in a field. The break crop often helps retain fertility.

pasture land put to grass and used for grazing.
permeable a soil or rock is permeable if it allows water to pass through it. It is **impermeable** if it doesn't allow water to pass through.

rotation a system of farming where a sequence of different crops are grown in a field to maintain fertility.
silage animal feed made from fermented grass, clover, etc.

10 Industry

A class of 11–12 year old pupils carried out a survey of their families' jobs. Some of the results are shown in Figure 1.

Pupil no	Job	Type
1	Vet	Tertiary
2	Shop Assistant	Tertiary
3	Taxi Driver	Tertiary
4	Gardener	Primary
5	Electrician	Secondary
6	Mechanic	Secondary

Figure 1 Parent job survey

If you study the last column carefully you will see that there are three types of job: **primary, secondary**, and **tertiary**. These are three basic types of industry.

- Primary Industry. This includes things like fishing, mining, agriculture. Because people in these kinds of job are extracting resources, primary is also called **extractive** industry.
- Secondary Industry. This involves actually making things and so is also called **manufacturing** industry. People who work in a car factory, or a steelworks or in a plant that makes computers will be employed in secondary industry.
- Tertiary Industry. Here people do not make anything but they provide a service. Shopkeepers, doctors, teachers, policemen, for example, are employed in serving the community in one way or another. Another name for this industry is **service** industry.

Primary: Forestry

Secondary: Manufacture of paper and board

Tertiary: Retailing of paper and cardboard products

Recycling

The three types of industry are often inter-linked. People working in **offices** who help to run and manage industry (like secretaries and directors) also work in the service sector. They cannot exist in total isolation (see Figure 2). Together they produce materials, goods and services to benefit society. This production is what **industry** is all about.

Figure 2

Activities

1 With the help of your teacher and your parents, draw up a table of jobs for your class like the one in Figure 1. Construct a bar chart to show the number of people working in each type of industry.

2 Your results to Activity 1 may show a concentration of one particular type of industry. Discuss the reasons why your locality may have this particular concentration.

3 Study Figure 2 which shows the links between the types of industry that are found associated with paper.
   a Describe the links in your own words.
   b Choose another set of industrial types that are closely linked and draw a diagram similar to the one in Figure 2.

10.2   The Location of Industry

A business must make a profit if it is to be successful. The cost of making something has to be less than the selling price. If it isn't, then the firm is going to lose money and possibly go bankrupt.

The position, or **location**, of a firm is very important in determining its success. The location of a firm is chosen so that all the firm's essential requirements can be brought together as cheaply as possible.

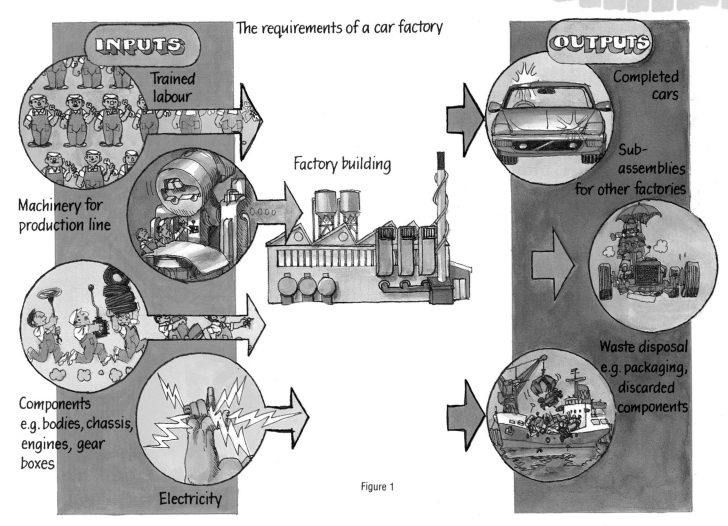

The requirements of a car factory

INPUTS
- Trained labour
- Machinery for production line
- Components e.g. bodies, chassis, engines, gear boxes
- Electricity

Factory building

OUTPUTS
- Completed cars
- Sub-assemblies for other factories
- Waste disposal e.g. packaging, discarded components

Figure 1

Figure 1 shows the requirements of a typical factory making motor cars. You will see that the factory has a number of **inputs** and a number of **outputs**.

Cars are heavy and difficult to transport in bulk. They are more expensive to transport than the components. Therefore the factory is more likely to be located closer to its customers than to its suppliers of components. This is an example of a **market orientated** industry.

Steel making on the other hand uses very heavy raw materials like iron ore, coke and limestone. These are more expensive to transport than the finished steel articles. For this reason steelworks tend to be located in a place where the raw materials can be easily brought together. Such an industry is called a **raw materials orientated** industry.

Some modern industries rely on a very skilled workforce, some of whom may be involved in **research and development**. 'High Tech' electronics, computers and scientific equipment are included here. These can be said to be **labour orientated**.

Tertiary industry uses a lot of labour and since it provides services it must be accessible to its market.

Some areas of the country are not very profitable places for modern industry to locate in, e.g. the North East or Northern Ireland. Such regions may not be very popular with people who manage industry. Therefore the Government tries to encourage firms by setting up **Development Areas**. These are areas where grants, loans and tax reductions are available to new firms. By encouraging industry in this way, the government hopes to reduce unemployment.

Activities

1 Choose a particular local industry and draw a diagram for it like the one shown in Figure 1. Don't forget to identify the inputs and the outputs.

2 Carefully study the information that is shown in Figure 2.

  a On an outline map of Britain, mark on all the steelworks, car factories and high technology areas. Write out the key and put the letters in the key next to the correct industries on your map. You will probably need an atlas to help you.

  b The major regions with dense population and receiving Government aid have been named. Write out a list of these names and next to each one write down the name of the main city or cities in that area. You may need to use your atlas.

  c Try to find out the name of the car manufacturer at each of the car factories marked on the map. Why are they so close to densely populated areas?

  d Explain why Teesside is a good place for a large, modern steelworks.

  e Study the photograph taken above a 'high-tech' park near Reading. Imagine you are one of the directors of a firm making computers. You are trying to persuade your fellow directors to build a new factory on the field in the middle of the picture. What evidence would you take from the photograph to convince your colleagues that the field is a good site?

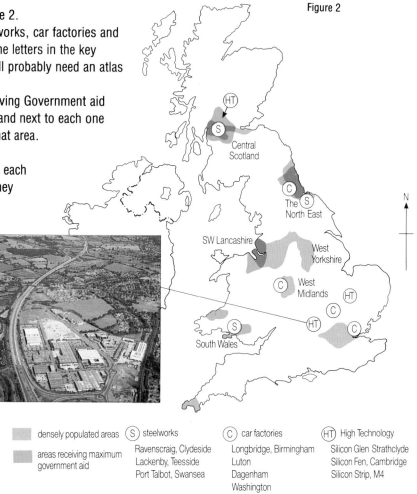

Figure 2

▓ densely populated areas	(S) steelworks	(C) car factories	(HT) High Technology
▓ areas receiving maximum government aid	Ravenscraig, Clydeside Lackenby, Teesside Port Talbot, Swansea	Longbridge, Birmingham Luton Dagenham Washington	Silicon Glen Strathclyde Silicon Fen, Cambridge Silicon Strip, M4

10.3 Salt in Cheshire: a Primary Industry

You may not realise that the salt you sprinkle over your chips at lunch may well be about 200 million years old! A lot of the salt we use was formed in large salt lakes when the area now called Cheshire had a hot desert climate. The salt extracted from the ground comes in two basic forms: **brine** and **rock salt**. Figure 1 shows how these are extracted. The map in Figure 2 shows where they are extracted in Cheshire.

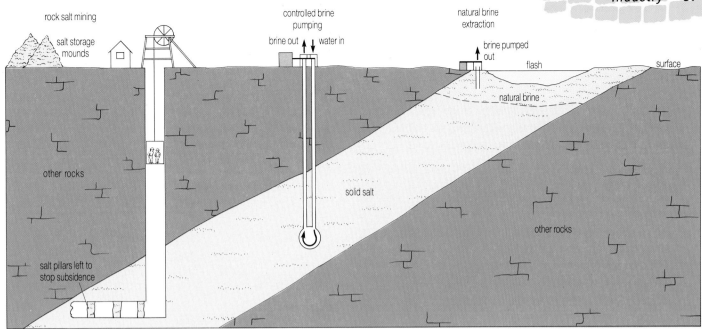

rock salt mining

salt storage mounds

controlled brine pumping

brine out ↑   ↓ water in

natural brine extraction

brine pumped out ↑

flash

surface

natural brine

other rocks

solid salt

other rocks

salt pillars left to stop subsidence

Figure 1

Figure 2

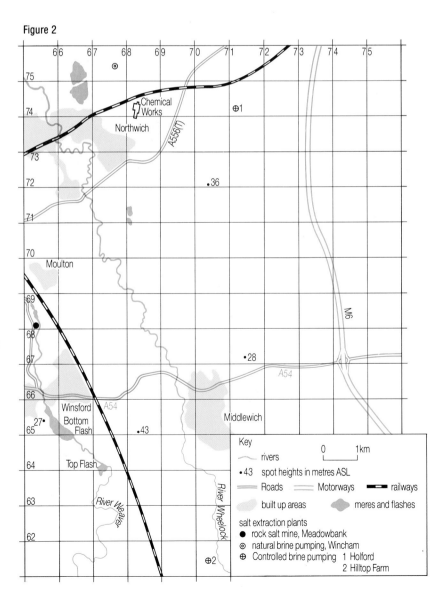

Key

rivers

0   1km

•43 spot heights in metres ASL

Roads   Motorways   railways

built up areas   meres and flashes

salt extraction plants

● rock salt mine, Meadowbank

◉ natural brine pumping, Wincham

⊕ Controlled brine pumping 1 Holford
2 Hilltop Farm

1 Brine.

Some of the salt beneath the surface has been dissolved naturally by the **ground water**. This dissolved salt, called brine, can be pumped up quite easily. Unfortunately the empty space left by the pumping out of the brine can cause the ground surface to **subside**. The hollows that form become flooded to produce **meres** and **flashes**. Some of these can be seen on the map in Figure 2.

In **controlled brine pumping** water is pumped into the solid salt. The water dissolves the salt which can then be pumped up. The ICI pumps at Holford produce more brine than anywhere else in the country. This method does not cause subsidence.

75% of the brine extracted is used in the chemical industry both in Cheshire and in other parts of the country. Caustic soda and chlorine are the chief products. The other 25% goes into white salt, used in foods.

2 Rock Salt.

This is solid salt. The mine at Winsford produces nearly all the country's requirements, and most of it is spread on the roads in winter to clear away snow and ice.

Activities

1 Figure 3 is a word search. Find as many of the words as you can. When you have found a word, write it in your exercise book and briefly describe in your own words what it has to do with the salt industry.

2 Look carefully at photographs A, and B in Figure 4. Answer the following questions:

Photograph A
a Do you think this shows a salt mine or a brine pump? Give reasons for your answer!
b What means of transport is used to take the salt away from the site?
c Make a sketch of the scene and label what you think are the important features.

Photograph B
a What method of salt extraction is shown in the photograph?
b What do you think the man in the photograph is doing?

3 Describe the effects that salt mines and brine pumps have on the countryside. Which one do you think is the most nuisance for the local people, and why?

4 Now look at the map shown in Figure 2.
a In which grid square is the rock salt mine located?
b Give the grid square for the Holford brine pump.
c What do you think is the nearest market shown on the map for the brine from Holford? How far away from Holford is this market?
d Bottom Flash (square 6665) is used for sailing. What reasons can you see from the map that make it a good lake for a sailing club?

5 Figure 5 is a bar graph that shows the output of rock salt from Cheshire between 1973 and 1983. Study this and then answer the following questions:
a What was the total output of rock salt between 1973 and 1983?
b What year had the lowest output, and how much was produced?
c What year had the highest output, and how much was produced?
d From what you read on page 87, say which years you think probably had mild winters and those that had cold winters. Give reasons for your answers.

6 Imagine your local authority has to buy some rock salt from the Meadowbank mine in Cheshire. With the help of your atlas, or a road atlas, write down the directions you would give to the lorry driver that has to go and collect the salt. How many kilometres would the driver travel on the round trip there and back? Draw a sketch map of the route he might take.

Figure 3

BRINE, CHEMICALS, CHESHIRE, FLASHES, ICE, MINE, MERES, PUMP, ROCK SALT, SODA, SUBSIDENCE, WINSFORD,

Figure 4

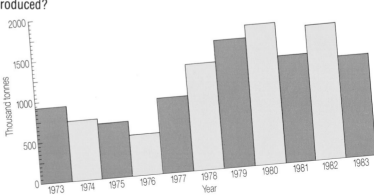

Figure 5

10.4 The Nissan car factory in North East England: a Secondary Industry

During the nineteenth century the North East of England (see Figure 1) developed rapidly. Coal mining, steel making, ship building and chemicals were the growth industries. However since the early days of this century these industries have declined. This has produced high unemployment, poverty for many people and derelict areas.

Nissan is one Japanese company that has been encouraged by the government to move into the region. It has established a car plant at Washington (see Figure 1) on the old airfield and by 1993 will be building 200 000 Bluebird cars per year and employing over 4 000 people, most of them local. Nissan chose Washington because of:

- financial incentives like grants and tax exemptions
- a convenient location for bringing in the components and exporting the assembled cars
- good labour relations in the area and the co-operation of the unions
- potential links with Durham and Newcastle Universities and the polytechnic at Sunderland.

Britain as a whole is attractive for Japanese investment. By making products here they can export to the rest of the European Community without having to pay the EC's import duties. Also, the Japanese learn English as their second language.

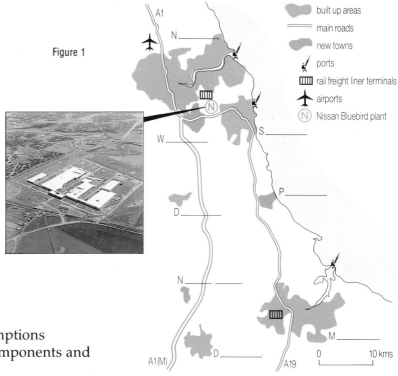

Figure 1

built up areas
main roads
new towns
ports
rail freight liner terminals
airports
(N) Nissan Bluebird plant

Figure 2:
Car Sales: Share of UK Market [%] 1989

Ford	18.0
Rover Group	16.0
Japanese	11.0 (Nissan has 58.0)
Vauxhall	8.0 (General Motors)
Peugeot	2.0
Other EC	40.0
Other UK	0.5
Rest	4.5

Activities

1 Make a copy of the map shown in Figure 1. Write in the names of the towns in the spaces provided. You will need your atlas!

2 Study Figure 1. Why do you think the old airfield is a good site for a car plant?

3 From the evidence in Figure 1 say why Washington is a convenient location for:
   - bringing in components and

   - the sale and export of cars.

4 Draw either a bar graph or a pie chart to show the figures in Figure 2. Can you think of some companies that make up the 'other EC' category?

5 Find out some of the other Japanese firms that have set up factories in Britain. Where are they located and what do they make?

10.5   Chester Business Park: Tertiary Industry

Space for new buildings in city centres is becoming scarce. This means that more and more new development is being put on the fringes of cities. Many modern businesses and offices are found in special areas called **business parks**. It is easier to provide buildings with things like gas, water, electricity and telephone lines if they are concentrated in one area. There are often special incentives from local and central government for firms wanting to establish offices in business parks.

Chester is trying to encourage business development. One of the major sites is the development on the southern side of the city: Chester Business Park. The Department of Trade and Industry is offering grants and financial assistance to companies wishing to come to Chester, which has full Development Area Status. Grants are available to firms for investment projects which create or safeguard jobs. Assistance can be given to firms for training costs. Grants are also available to support joint research projects with universities. The European Investment Bank may also provide loans.

Activities

1 Turn to the OS map extract of Chester on page 108. Find the site of the Business Park at 395628. Note that it has not yet been marked on the map. Now answer the following questions:

a Draw a sketch map of the extract and mark on the following:
   Central Business District of Chester
   built-up areas   'A' roads
   river   Chester Business Park
   Do not forget to give your map a title, key and scale.

b How many kilometres is it from the Business Park to the bus station in the city centre?

c Describe the relief of the land at the site of the Business Park.

d Why are sites like this called 'greenfield sites'?

2 Look carefully at the aerial photograph in Figure 1 which shows the site of the Business Park. You will also need to refer to the OS map again.

a In which direction is the camera pointing?

b What is the building that is located between the corner of the Business Park and the intersection of the A55 and A483 (T)?

c Name the housing area that can be seen in the top left of the photograph.

3 Now read the information in Figure 1.

a How big is the Business Park?

b What are the 'prestige' companies already established there? What types of industry do they represent? (Refer back to page 83).

4 What advantages does the Business Park have for

a a firm that exports to Europe;

b an executive that regularly has to fly to New York on business;

c an employee with a teenage family.

5 Design a poster that could be used to advertise the advantages of Chester Business Park for office development. Newspapers often carry such advertisements – your class could collect some and make a wall display.

6 Is there a similar new business park in your local area? If so, find out:

a its location,

b the firms that are found there,

c the help (if any) that firms can receive from the local authority or the government.
   Design a brochure giving details of your local business park and advertising the advantages of locating there.

Figure 1

GREAT COMMUNICATIONS

CHESTER IS VERY well connected by road, rail and air. Just to the north, the M53 motorway links with the M56 heading East. This motorway in turn meets the M6 which provides access North and South.

All the major centres of the Midlands can be reached in around an hour with Liverpool and Manchester being within 40 minutes by car.

Even London is just over 3 hours drive away. Chester is also on the Inter City Rail Network, with frequent services to Birmingham (1 hour), London (2½ hours) and Glasgow (4½ hours). Manchester International Airport, which is the largest in the UK outside of London, is 30 minutes away from Chester by car.

ALREADY A SUCCESS STORY

CHESTER BUSINESS PARK occupies a total of 150 acres fringed by the main A55 ring road. Already, 250 000 square feet of the 1 million square feet of office accommodation has been constructed. Superb offices have already been built for Marks & Spencer, Shell Chemicals and Videcom.

Other national and international companies are close behind, taking a long look at the first class communications and low cost of living.

As an added incentive, Chester also has full development area status, which opens the door to Government and EC financial assistance.

YOU WON'T FIND A BETTER LOCATION

CHESTER'S HISTORY STRETCHES right back to Roman and Medieval times. Within these walls are many timber framed buildings from the 17th Century, including its elegant 'Rows' of galleried shops. There is also a famous Cathedral which originates from 992 AD.

Add the modern shopping centres and many leisure activities of this thriving area, and it's no surprise that many visitors descend on Chester every year – nor that so many people would like to live and work here.

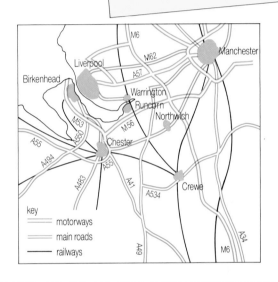

Dictionary

business park an area devoted to office development.

controlled brine pumping injection of water into salt deposits below the ground dissolving the salt to be pumped to the surface.

development areas areas designated by the government to receive financial aid.

ground water water that exists naturally in rocks under the ground.

industry production of goods and services.

industrial estate an estate of factories.

inputs things that go into a system.

labour orientated industry located near its workers.

location position.

manufacturing the making of goods.

market orientated industry located near its market.

meres and flashes flooded areas produced by the subsidence of the land after mining.

outputs things that come out of a system.

primary first type of industry, also called extractive e.g. mining

raw materials orientated industry located near its supply of raw materials.

research and development the investigation of new ideas and projects for industry.

secondary second type of industry, also known as manufacturing e.g. television sets.

service industrial activity assisting other activities and people e.g. banking.

subside to sink, as in land subsidence after mining.

tertiary third type of industry also known as services (see above).

11 Recreation

Today we all have much more spare time than we would have had 20 years ago. Many of us choose to fill our spare time with sports and hobbies – these are forms of **recreation**.

Recreation can be active and organised (**formal**), e.g. playing football or tennis, or it can be more relaxed and **informal**, e.g. walking, picnicking, birdwatching. Simply sitting in a nice area of countryside is recreation.

Look at the photographs in Figure 1. They show forms of recreation in a park. A map of the park is shown in and you can see where each of the photographs was taken.

Sometimes there is **conflict** between different forms of recreation. For example, car racing and birdwatching do not go together very well! Planners have to try and avoid conflicts to make sure that everybody is kept happy.

Figure 1

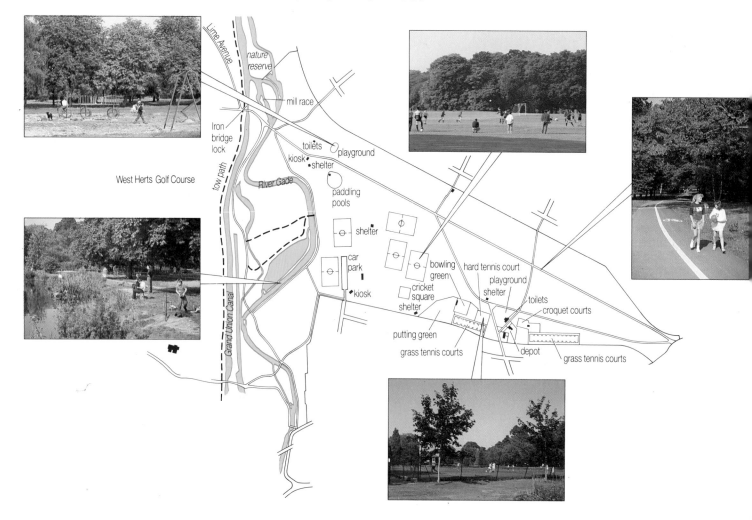

Activities

1 Study the photographs in Figure 1. For each photograph:
   a Describe the environment (e.g. playing fields, water, wood, rough grass).
   b Describe the forms of recreation taking place. Are they **formal**, **informal** or a mixture?

2 In pairs, make a list of as many recreational activities as you can that might take place on or beside a reservoir. Use your list to help you complete the table in Figure 2.

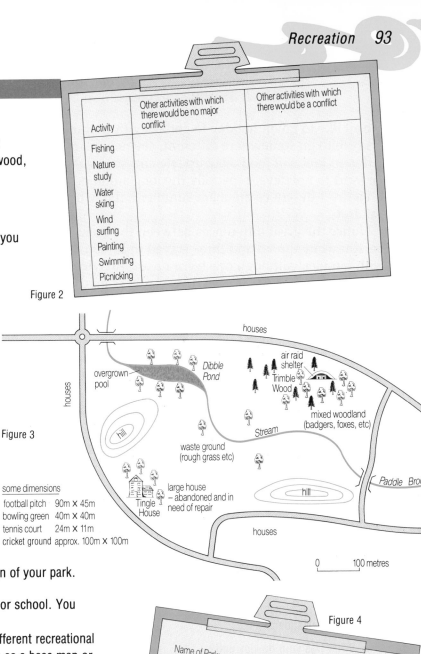

Activity	Other activities with which there would be no major conflict	Other activities with which there would be a conflict
Fishing		
Nature study		
Water skiing		
Wind surfing		
Painting		
Swimming		
Picnicking		

Figure 2

Figure 3

some dimensions
football pitch 90m × 45m
bowling green 40m × 40m
tennis court 24m × 11m
cricket ground approx. 100m × 100m

3 In this activity you will be planning a park of your own. Figure 3 shows a piece of vacant land on the edge of a town which you have been asked to turn into a park for the people of the town.
   a Make a list of those activities and forms of recreation that you want to cater for. Use Figure 1 to help you.
   b Make a **rough** plan of your park. Draw the outline of the park from Figure 3. Locate your chosen forms of recreation and add any landscape features such as trees and water. You must also have one or more car parks, information boards, and toilets.
   c When you are happy with your rough version, complete your final map. Take time to make it attractive and clear. Give your park a name.
   d Write a short account giving the reasons for the design of your park.

4 Make a study of recreation in a park close to your home or school. You could do the following:
   a Make a map of the park showing the location of the different recreational activities. You could use a local Ordnance Survey map as a base map or you could produce your own **mental map** (see page 2).
   b Interview some of the park users. Figure 4 shows some of the questions you might ask people. Try to ask a range of different people and, as a class, try to ask at least 50 in total.
      Your results could be displayed as bar graphs or pie charts. Use a **sphere of influence** to show where people have come from to visit the park.
   c Suggest additions or alterations to the park. Give reasons for your suggestions.

5 On a base map of your home town locate the various recreation facilities – include both formal facilities such as sports halls and informal facilities such as parks. Use colours to make your map clearer. You might like to use different colours to show 'formal' and 'informal' facilities. Is your town well served or are other facilities needed? If so, what is/are needed and where should it/they be located?

Figure 4

Name of Park: _____
Date of Survey: _____
Time of Survey: _____

1 Where have you come from to visit the park?

2 What have you come to do in the park?
walk ☐   walk dog ☐   picnic ☐   football ☐
tennis ☐   bowls ☐   other _____

3 How have you travelled to the park today?
walk ☐   car ☐   cycle ☐   bus ☐
train ☐   other _____

4 How frequently do you visit the park?
daily ☐   2-3 times a week ☐   once a week ☐
2-3 times a month ☐   less often ☐

5 Are you satisfied with the park facilities?
excellent ☐   good ☐   satisfactory ☐   could be better ☐

6 How could the park facilities be improved? _____

11.2 Holidays

We all like to go on holiday to get away from the daily routine. It's nice to go somewhere different, see new places, eat different kinds of food, stay up late and so on. We look forward to holidays, especially the long summer holiday.

Figure 1 describes the main summer holiday taken by 4 children.

Notice the great differences between the holidays taken. One person went abroad and three stayed in Britain. Most went with families, although one went on an 'Activity' holiday. One holiday was 'sand and sea' whereas others involved touring. The accommodation varied – camping, self catering and hotels.

We can see that when studying holidays we need to consider the following aspects:

- The nature of the **holiday unit** (e.g. family, friends, single)
- The holiday **destination** (e.g. Blackpool, Spain, France, Isle of Wight).
- The **accommodation** (e.g. self-catering, hotel, guest house, camping).
- The **type** of holiday (e.g. sand and sea, touring, visiting friends).

> I went to Spain with my Mum, Dad, brother and sister. We stayed in a hotel near Alicante. On most days we went to the beach or stayed by the hotel swimming pool.

> I spent 2 weeks at an Activity Holiday Centre in Wales. I learned to canoe and windsurf which was well good.

> My little brother and I went camping in Yorkshire with Dad. As we're all interested in trains we visited steam railways and the Railway Museum in York.

> We hired a cottage in Devon for a week. The roof leaked but it didn't matter! We saw the Dartmoor ponies and spent a couple of days on the coast.

Figure 1

Activities

1 Carry out a study of the main summer holiday taken by members of your class.

To do this, each member of the class should write down answers to the following questions:

- What was your holiday **unit**?
- What was your **destination**?
- What was the main type of **accommodation**?
- What **type** of holiday was it?

Now you need to make a copy of the whole class's answers.

This information now needs to be turned into diagram form to make it clearer and more interesting to look at. Figure 2 shows how **flow lines** can be used to show destinations. Use **bars** and **pies** to show the other information.

Produce diagrams of your choice. Take time to produce colourful, clear and attractive diagrams.

Write up your study as follows:

- Give your study a suitable heading.
- Describe how the information was obtained and include **your** answers to the four questions.
- Show the class results using diagrams of your choice.
- Describe the **trends** shown by the results.
  (It would be a good idea to discuss this as a class first.)

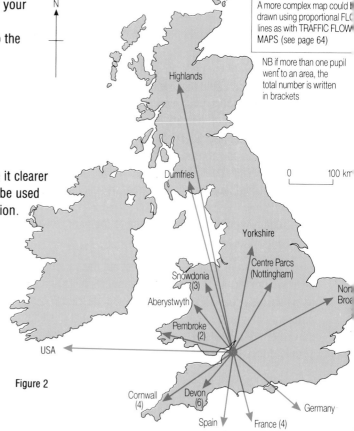

A more complex map could be drawn using proportional FLOW lines as with TRAFFIC FLOW MAPS (see page 64)

NB if more than one pupil went to an area, the total number is written in brackets

Figure 2

2 Read the newspaper article Figure 3. It describes recent British holiday trends.

   a Why are 'More people than ever staying at home'?

   b What groups of people will be pleased with this fact and why?

   c What are tour operators doing to try and get more Britons to travel abroad?

3 Figure 4 shows where the 'home' British holidays were taken in 1988. Attempt the following questions in pairs or in small groups. An atlas may help you.

   a Which was the most popular holiday destination in Britain? What percentage of holidaymakers went there?

   b Why do you think this area was so popular?

   c Which was the most popular part of Wales visited? What does this area offer to the holidaymaker?

   d The **Highlands and Islands** were the most popular part of Scotland visited. Why do you think this was so?

4 For this Activity you will need to work in pairs or in small groups.

Your job is to produce a tourist brochure for your local area. It is up to you to decide how large an area to cover – you could cover the whole of your County or just part of it. You could cover your home town only.

Carry out some research to find out what there is of interest in your chosen area. Visit your library, a local Tourist Information Centre if you have one, look through local newspaper and ask your family and friends.

Your brochure should be no larger than a double-sided A3 sheet. It should be clear and colourful and should stress the different attractions of your area. A map would be essential. Decide what to do as a group and then each one take on a particular job.

More Britons are staying at home for holidays
By Robert Bedlow

AIRPORT CHAOS and flight delays, high interest rates and mortgage repayments are putting the British holidaymaker off foreign travel, according to the British Tourist Authority. "More people than ever are staying at home," it said yesterday.

Statistics showed that the three-year decline in the number of Britons holidaying in the United Kingdom was reversed last year.

An estimated 39 per cent of British adults last year spent four nights or more on holiday in this country, an increase of eight per cent over 1987 while the proportion holidaying abroad was unchanged at 30 per cent.

A BTA spokesman said: "Many people have been put off by the airport delays. But there is no doubt that the higher interest and mortgage repayments are having their effect.

A record 24 per cent of the population spent more than one long holiday, four nights or more, in Britain. In all, Britons took 53-75 million long holidays in 1988 with 33-5 million at home and 20-25 million overseas.

"These are heartening figures and there is every indication that 1989 will be a good year, too," the spokesman said.

Already major leading tour operators have been forced to cut their overseas holiday programmes because of the lack of business. Some have slashed prices and offered other incentives in an attempt to boost flagging sales.

But figures from the English Tourist Board for 1989 so far show increase of between 10 and 50 per cent on all kinds of holidays in England.

Daily Telegraph 29.3.89

Figure 3

Scale percentage of total holidays

10%

5%

0%

(1cm = 5%)

0   100 kms

Scotland

rest of Scotland

Highlands and Islands

Northumbria

Cumbria

Yorkshire and Humberside

North West

Mid Wales

South Wales

North Wales

Wales

Heart of England

East Anglia

Thames and Chiltern

London

Southern

South East

West Country

Figure 4

National parks

A **National Park** is an area of beautiful and often dramatic countryside which is protected from large scale development. There are 10 **National Parks** in England and Wales (see Figure 1). Each National Park is looked after by a Park Authority. Its job is to protect the countryside and the people who live there as well as encouraging recreational use of the area.

There is sometimes conflict between the different land users. Some organisations may wish to use land for military training, quarrying, or the development of new roads. Tourism itself can be harmful to the countryside as litter is left behind, footpaths become trampled and **eroded**, fires may be started and farm animals worried by dogs not kept on leads.

Planning a National Park is a very difficult job if everybody is to be satisfied.

In 1989, The Broads was given the same status as a National Park making it the eleventh large area of protected land in England and Wales. The Broads Authority is very similar to but not exactly the same as a National Park.

Figure 1

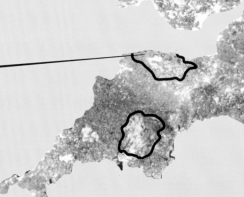

1 a On an outline of England and Wales (a tracing of Figure 1 will do) draw the extent of each National Park.
  b Use the shapes given in Figure 2 to identify the name of each park and write these onto your map as labels.
  c Using an atlas, locate on your map the following major cities: London; Birmingham; Norwich; Bristol; Plymouth; Cardiff; Manchester; Sheffield; Leeds; Newcastle-upon-Type.

2 Use your map completed in Activity 1 to answer the following questions:
  a Which National Park is close to Norwich?
  b Which National Parks include a stretch of coastline?
  c Which National Park is close to several large cities? Suggest some problems that you might expect to find in this National Park.
  d Why are most National Parks in the west and north of England and Wales? (An atlas may help you with this question.)
  e Which part of England and Wales does not have any National Parks? Why do you think this is so? (An atlas may help you with this question.)

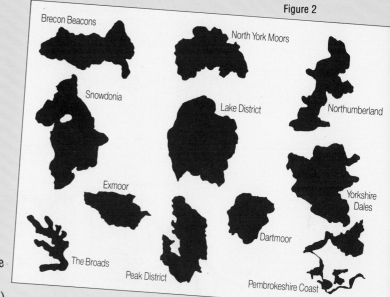

Figure 2

Brecon Beacons
North York Moors
Snowdonia
Lake District
Northumberland
Exmoor
Yorkshire Dales
The Broads
Dartmoor
Peak District
Pembrokeshire Coast

3 Discuss as a class the characteristics of National Parks. To do this you should share your own experiences of visiting National Parks. Describe to others what a National Park is like. What does it **look** like? What does it **feel** like (peaceful? calming? exciting?)? Use the photographs in Figure 1 to help.
You may find it useful to make some rough notes during the discussion to remind you of some of the characteristics.
Now choose one of the following pieces of work to do:
  a Write a poem about the beauty of National Parks.
  b Write a short piece under the title 'Why National Parks should be protected from development'.
  c Imagine that you live in a National Park (some of you might!). There is a proposal to turn part of the park into a military training area.
  Either – Write a letter to your local newspaper giving your views about the proposal.
  Or – Produce a campaign poster against this proposal. The poster should include a sketch or cartoon and a clear, simple slogan.

11.4 Recreation in Dartmoor National Park

Spend some time looking at the information in Figure 1. Locate Dartmoor in an atlas. Notice that it is between the two cities of Exeter and Plymouth.

Dartmoor consists of varied scenery as Figure 1 shows. To the north, the High Moor is bleak and desolate granite moorland. To the south, the landscape is more rolling with steep river valleys.

The combination of moorland, river valleys, reservoirs and historic towns means that Dartmoor can offer a great range of recreational experiences.

Figure 1

Dartmoor National Park

Activities

1 In pairs, use Figure 1 to make a list of the range of recreational activities available in Dartmoor National Park.

2 Imagine that you are working for the South Devon Tourist Board in Exeter. A middle aged American couple ask your advice about where to go to see some of the main sites on Dartmoor. They give the following information to help you:

They have a small car.
They like castles and other ancient buildings.
They don't mind short strolls to viewing points but they don't want long hikes.
They can spend two full days in the area (including two nights).
They have friends in Buckfastleigh and would like to spend one of the two nights there.
Most importantly of all, they want to see a variety of landscapes.

Normally you would give them a few booklets but, as you suspect a large tip might be offered, you decide to give them a detailed plan for their two days!

Produce a plan (called an **itinerary**) for the two days. You should include a route map for each of the two days with the main 'points of interest' either written onto the map or in a separate section. Remember to state where they should stay on each of the two nights and that on one night they wish to stay in Buckfastleigh.

Bear in mind that travelling is very slow as roads are narrow and busy. A 30 mile round trip in one day is about the limit — otherwise, your Americans will be spending far too long in the car.

3 If *you* were to visit Dartmoor but you only had a single day, where would you go and what would you want to do? Give some reasons for your answer.

4 Look at Figure 2. It shows one of the many problems resulting from people's use of National parks. In pairs or small groups, make a list of some of the problems created by people in visiting National Parks.

Figure 2

Dictionary

formal recreation organised activities often involving teams such as football

holiday break from the normal routine often involving travelling away from home

informal recreation non-organised activities such as walking
National Park protected area of great natural beauty.

12.1 What is an ecosystem

All animals and plants are linked together with the natural environment (soil, weather) – this is called an **ecosystem** (see Figure 1). As all the different parts of an ecosystem are linked together, a change in one will often cause a change in the others. For example, cutting down and burning the rainforests causes the soil to become infertile and the atmosphere to warm up (the '**greenhouse effect**').

The ecosystem described above is the **global ecosystem**. There are, however, many smaller ecosystems, e.g. a pond, a wood or a salt marsh.

For hundreds, if not thousands of years people have exploited the environment without realising the effect on ecosystems. Plants and animals have become extinct as a result. You can, therefore, see how important it is for us to understand ecosystems and to know how easily they can be damaged.

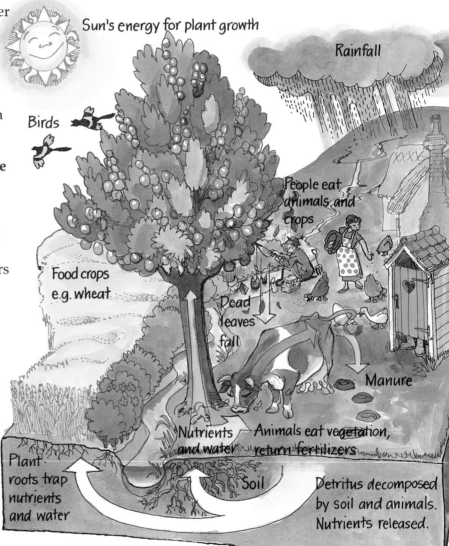

Sun's energy for plant growth

Rainfall

Birds

People eat animals and crops

Food crops e.g. wheat

Dead leaves fall

Manure

Nutrients and water

Animals eat vegetation, return fertilizers

Plant roots trap nutrients and water

Soil

Detritus decomposed by soil and animals. Nutrients released.

Figure 1

Activities

1 Study Figure 1.
  a What characteristics of the weather are shown on Figure 1?
  b Can you think of any other important weather characteristics that are not shown?
  c Why do plants have roots?
  d What happens to fallen leaves?
  e What would happen to the ecosystem if the trees were chopped down?
  f In some parts of the world animal manure is burned as a fuel. What effect would you expect this to have on the ecosystem?

2 a Make a large copy of Figure 2.
  b Figure 3 contains a number of different parts of
    an ecosystem. Draw these in sensible positions
    on your copy of Figure 2.

Figure 3

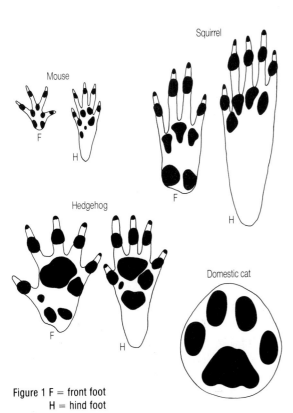

Figure 2

12.2   *Studying wildlife in the local environment*

It is not difficult to study wildlife in gardens or in the school grounds. It is just a matter of opening our eyes and looking closely at, for example, flower beds or grassy areas.

This unit contains a number of suggestions for you to make your own study of a local environment. Your study could be done on your own or in small groups.

Remember that it is your job to look after anything you find and return it to the wild. Do not pick wild flowers and be careful not to harm small and delicate animals.

It is strongly recommended that you make use of some reference books perhaps borrowed from your school or local library.

1 Studying tracks

You have probably seen tracks left by animals in newly fallen snow. Cats and birds leave very distinctive tracks. However, you do not have to wait for a fall of snow to find tracks – try looking at newly dried mud at the edge of puddles or on grass with a dew on it.

The tracks in Figure 1 and Figure 5 are quite common and will help you to identify some of those you find. Use sketches to show the tracks you discover and measure the distance between the prints to discover the length of stride.

Mouse

Squirrel

Hedgehog

Domestic cat

Figure 1 F = front foot
         H = hind foot

2 Studying bugs

The ground surface is alive with little bugs some of which are shown in Figure 2. You can study these and other bugs by sinking a small plastic beaker into the soil so that the top is just below the level of the ground surface. Make a few small holes at the bottom of your beaker to allow any rainwater to drain away and so prevent small creatures drowning.

Study the contents of your beaker daily to examine any inmates. Keep a record of what you find – types of creature and numbers. Use sketches and measurements if possible. Remember to treat all creatures with great care and *always* release them back into the wild.

It would be interesting to place beakers in several different places to see which areas were most popular with bugs. Try to suggest why this is the case.

3 Studying nuts and seeds

Nuts and seeds are important sources of protein, oil and starch for birds and small animals. Close examination around the base of a tree can sometimes reveal evidence of feasting (see Figure 3).

Study the bases of several trees and keep a record of what you find. You could relate your results to the type or size of the tree – Figure 4 illustrates some common types of tree.

Figure 2
Wolf spider
Earwig
Woodlice
Millipede

Pine cones

A pine cone eaten by a squirrel becomes frayed. They are nearly always found out in the open

A cone eaten by a mouse has more tidily gnawed scales and the cones are found in sheltered places

A cone attacked by a woodpecker. The scales are split longways

Hazelnuts

An adult squirrel gnaws a small hole in the top and levers the nut open with its teeth

A young squirrel gnaws all over the nut until a hole appears

A mouse usually attacks the side of the nut

Great tit: most nuts eaten by birds show beak marks on the smooth brown surface

Figure 3

Figure 4   Sitka spruce   Oak   Birch   Beech   Poplar

4 *Birdwatching*

This study is best done during the winter months as during the summer food is plentiful and birds do not need feeders.

Some of you may be keen birdwatchers. If so, you will know how patient you have to be in order to spot interesting birds.

Find a relatively quiet spot in your garden or at school to set up a birdfeeder. These can be bought fairly cheaply from most garden centres or from the RSPB. Hang your feeder from a low branch of a tree – make sure that you can see it from a window! Wait a few days for the birds to get used to the new object (they won't visit it straight away) and then keep a record of the types of birds that visit. If you are unfamiliar with common birds, make use of a reference book

It is possible to combine many of the smaller studies described above into one large study. You could study the wildlife in a small area for a week or two making records of what you see and find. You could illustrate your project with photographs and sketches and you could use a map or plan to show the layout of your study area.

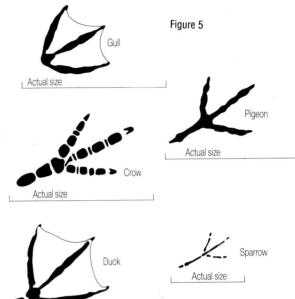

Figure 5

Gull
Actual size

Pigeon
Actual size

Crow
Actual size

Duck
Actual size

Sparrow
Actual size

12.3   Wildlife in derelict areas

Most towns have derelict areas. They might be former industrial areas or might border canals, roads and railways. At first sight these areas often seem to have no wildlife at all. This may be true but, with a little careful planning and planting, such areas can be transformed into small wildlife **habitats**.

Figure 1 shows an area of derelict land near Kings Cross Station in London. Figure 2 shows what it looks like now. Quite a transformation isn't it? The Camley Street Natural Park, as it is now known, contains a large pond, meadow and woodland providing a natural home for frogs, bees, birds and butterflies as well as many different plants. People from the local area visit the Park to enjoy its beauty.

Figure 1

Figure 2

Activities

1 The Camley Street Natural Park is run by the London Wildlife Trust. You have been asked to help the Trust in the following ways:-

   a By producing an information sheet for visitors to the park. It should be a single sheet of A4 paper and should contain:-
- a short history of the Park
- a brief outline of the aims of the Park
- some details of what to look for in the Park. Use diagrams to illustrate your sheet. Figure 3 gives you some important details.

   b By writing a local radio advert or designing a newspaper advert to inform local people about the Park.

What is Camley Street Natural Park?

Camley Street Natural Park is a place for people and wildlife. It's managed by London Wildlife Trust with support from Camden Council and local volunteers. Situated in Kings Cross and surrounded by the Regent's Canal, the busy streets and railways of Kings Cross and St Pancras, Camley Street provides two unique acres of open space in the centre of one of the world's largest capitals. Special features of the park include a large pond, meadows and woodland. These have been painstakingly created to provide a natural environment for birds, bees, butterflies, frogs and toads as well as a rich variety of plant life.

Camley Street's History

The history of Camley Street has come almost full circle since 1066 when the area was covered by the Middlesex Forest. That rich deciduous woodland gave way to settlements and cornfields as London expanded. By the 1400s the marshy area of Camley Street was surrounded by enclosures. As London grew the area fell into disuse until work began on the Regent's Canal, which was opened in the early 1820s.

With the canal came trade, and Camley Street itself was transformed into a huge coal storage area. The coal was transported from the north of England on canal barges. The population of the area grew rapidly, but with the sudden decline of the canal industry due to the arrival of the railways the area became the notorious slum of "Agar Town", described by Charles Dickens in Dombey & Son.

The gasholders visible from the park were built in the late 1800s by the Imperial Gas Light and Coke Company. They are still in use and now form as much a part of the local landscape as the park itself. More recently the site was used as an unofficial rubbish tip. Then the GLC stepped in and, after discarding plans for a coach park on the site, began creation of Camley Street Natural Park in late 1983. By mid 1984 the park had taken shape.

Figure 3

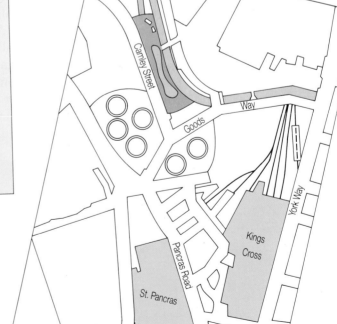

2 Design and set up your own 'natural park' perhaps in your school grounds. This is a large project and will take careful planning. It would be sensible to involve the Science Department at your school, particularly the biologists. Figure 4 gives some practical suggestions about how to set up your own natural area.

3 Figure 5 shows a derelict area. Work in pairs to suggest what could be done to improve this area both for wildlife and for people. Your main aim should be to provide a range of different habitats in order to encourage a variety of wildlife to the area. You need to plan for people too - car parks, picnic areas and nature trails, for example.

Produce a sketch map to show your suggestions.

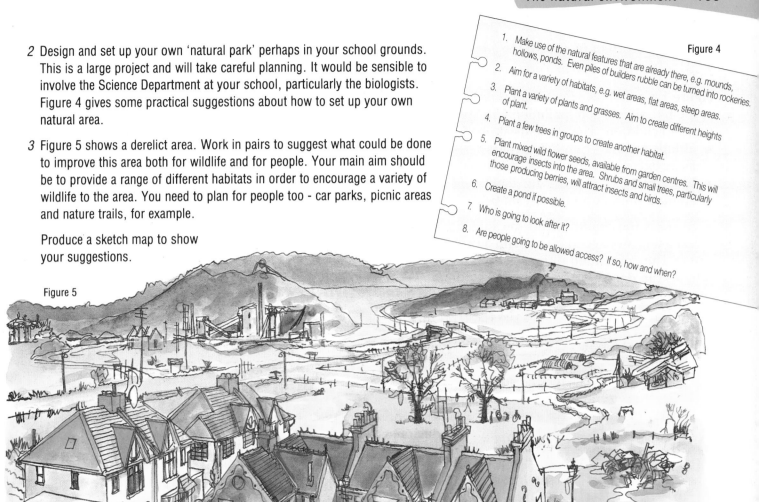

Figure 4

1. Make use of the natural features that are already there, e.g. mounds, hollows, ponds. Even piles of builders rubble can be turned into rockeries.
2. Aim for a variety of habitats, e.g. wet areas, flat areas, steep areas.
3. Plant a variety of plants and grasses. Aim to create different heights of plant.
4. Plant a few trees in groups to create another habitat.
5. Plant mixed wild flower seeds, available from garden centres. This will encourage insects into the area. Shrubs and small trees, particularly those producing berries, will attract insects and birds.
6. Create a pond if possible.
7. Who is going to look after it?
8. Are people going to be allowed access? If so, how and when?

Figure 5

12.4 Pollution in a small stream

Many streams and rivers contain human and industrial pollution. This includes sewage, metals and chemicals. These pollutants can have serious effects on our drinking water and on the stream ecosystem causing death to plants, fish and other organisms living in or by water.

One of the main pollutants of streams throughout the world is **sewage**. This includes:

- Urea (from our urine) which turns into harmful nitrates.
- Solid waste.
- Detergents, which may contain dangerous chemicals.

- Material waste, such as nappies.

Raw sewage is treated at **treatment works**. Here the sewage is screened, allowed to settle and finally bacteria act to break down the remaining substances. The remaining liquid waste can then be released into streams and rivers without having any harmful effects. Unfortunately, the process does not always work and streams and rivers do occasionally suffer. One common problem involves bacteria in the stream feeding on the sewage. This 'breakdown' of the sewage substances leads to a reduction in the oxygen content of the water and can lead to the death of fish.

Studying pollution in a small stream:
Pocklington Beck, North Yorkshire

Figure 1 maps shows Pocklington Beck and shows the location of the five sites where pollution was studied by a group of 12 year old children. The students studied two aspects:

- **abiotic factors** – non-living characteristics of the water, such as its oxygen level;
- **biotic factors** – living characteristics of the water, such as the animals present on the stream bed.

To study the abiotic factors the students recorded oxygen levels using an oxygen meter with a probe dipped into the water. They measured nitrate levels (in high concentrations nitrates can damage human health) by dipping special indicator paper (**Mercoquant Test strips**) into the water. This paper turns different shades of purple and a colour chart is used to estimate the concentration of dissolved nitrates. Three readings of oxygen and nitrates were taken at each site and the average calculated.

In studying biotic factors, the students used a technique called **kick-sampling**. This involves kicking or disturbing the river bed just upstream of a net for about 20 seconds. Larger stones are checked by hand. The animals which have been disturbed will then be caught in the net and can be studied by tipping them out into a tray half full of water. It is important not to harm any of the animals.

Figure 2 illustrates some of the more common animals found in streams. Some can only survive in very clean water whereas others can live in polluted water. Generally speaking, the greater the variety and the number of animals, the less polluted a stream. You can see, therefore, how a study of the animals in a stream can suggest to us how polluted the stream is. Figure 3 gives the results of the surveys carried out on the Pocklington Beck.

hills – some rough grazing and arable farming

Pocklington (population 10 000)

sewage works

Study sites
1   2 km upstream of sewage works
2   just below sewage outflow
3   200 m below sewage works
4   1 km below sewage works
5   2 km below sewage works

0 _____ 1 km

Figure 1

Figure 2

Cased Caddis Larva

Small Diving Beetle (Hydroporus)

Fresh Water Shrimp (Gammarus)

Olive Ma Nymph

Sludge Worm (Tubifex)

Chironomid Larva (Bloodworm)

Animals below the line can tolerate polluted water. Those above cannot.

1. ABIOTIC FACTORS

Factors	Site 1	Site 2	Site 3	Site 4	Site 5
Oxygen levels (mg1^{-1})	10.5	7.0	5.0	5.5	9.0
Nitrate levels (mg1^{-1})	50	50	100	100	50

(Three readings were taken at each site and an average calculated)

Figure 3

2. BIOTIC FACTORS

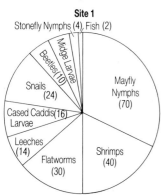

Site 1
Stonefly Nymphs (4), Fish (2)
Midge Larvae
Beetles (10)
Snails (24)
Cased Caddis (16) Larvae
Leeches (14)
Flatworms
Mayfly Nymphs (70)
Shrimps (40)

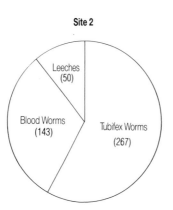

Site 2
Leeches (50)
Blood Worms (143)
Tubifex Worms (267)

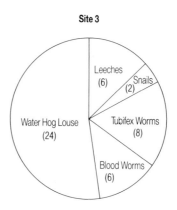

Site 3
Leeches (6)
Snails (2)
Water Hog Louse (24)
Tubifex Worms (8)
Blood Worms (6)

Site 4:
Water hog louse (40), Midge larvae (34), Snails (10), Leeches (4), Shrimps (12), Tubifex worms (20).

Site 5:
Shrimps (75) Mayfly nymphs, 2 species (50), Blackfly larvae (10), Fish (10), Midge larvae (30), Beetles, 2 species (20), snails (5).

Activities

1 Why do you think three readings of abiotic factors were taken at each site rather than just one?

2 a Draw a line graph to show how the abiotic values change with distance downstream. Figure 4 shows how to do this. Use arrows to show the approximate position of the town and the sewage works.
  b At which site was the oxygen level lowest? Why do you think this was so?
  c Had the oxygen levels fully recovered by site 5?
  d Use the map in Figure 1 to help you account for the already quite high concentrations of nitrates in the stream at site 1.
  e Use Figure 1 to help you explain the drop in the nitrates concentration between sites 4 and 5.

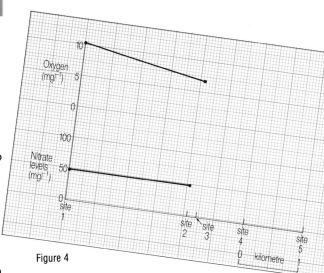

Figure 4

3 Draw pie charts to show the results of the biotic surveys at sites 4 and 5. To discover how many degrees each animal represents, you need to divide the number of each animal by the total number of all animals and multiply by 360. For example, for water hog louse at site 4:

number of water hog louse (40) divided by the total number of animals at site 4 (120) = 0.33 multiplied by 360 = 120 degrees.

You may need to round figures up or down so that you end up with 360 degrees in total. Your teacher will help you with this.

Use colours to shade your pie graphs.

4 a Copy and complete the table in Figure 5. Site 5 has been done for you.
  b Do you think the sewage works is polluting the stream? What evidence is there for this?
  c Why do you think there are actually more animals at site 2 than at site 3?
  d Do you think the animal community has completely recovered by site 5? Explain your answer.
  e What can you conclude about stonefly nymphs?
  f What can you conclude about leeches, bloodworms and Tubifex worms?
  g Why do you think there were no bloodworms at sites 1, 4 and 5?
  h Look back at Figure 1. Is it fair to just blame the sewage works for the pollution of Pocklington Beck?

Figure 5

	Site 1	Site 2	Site 3	Site 4	Site 5
Total abundance (number of animals)					200
Species Richness (number of different kinds of animals)					9
Dominant Animal (the most common animal at that site)					Shrimps

Dictionary

abiotic non-living characteristics
biotic living characteristics
ecosystem the interaction of all living things (plants, animals, etc) with the environment

greenhouse effect the warming of the earth's atmosphere
habitat a place that provides a particular set of environmental conditions for living things e.g. a pond or a hedge.

pollution presence in the environment of harmful or unpleasant substances.

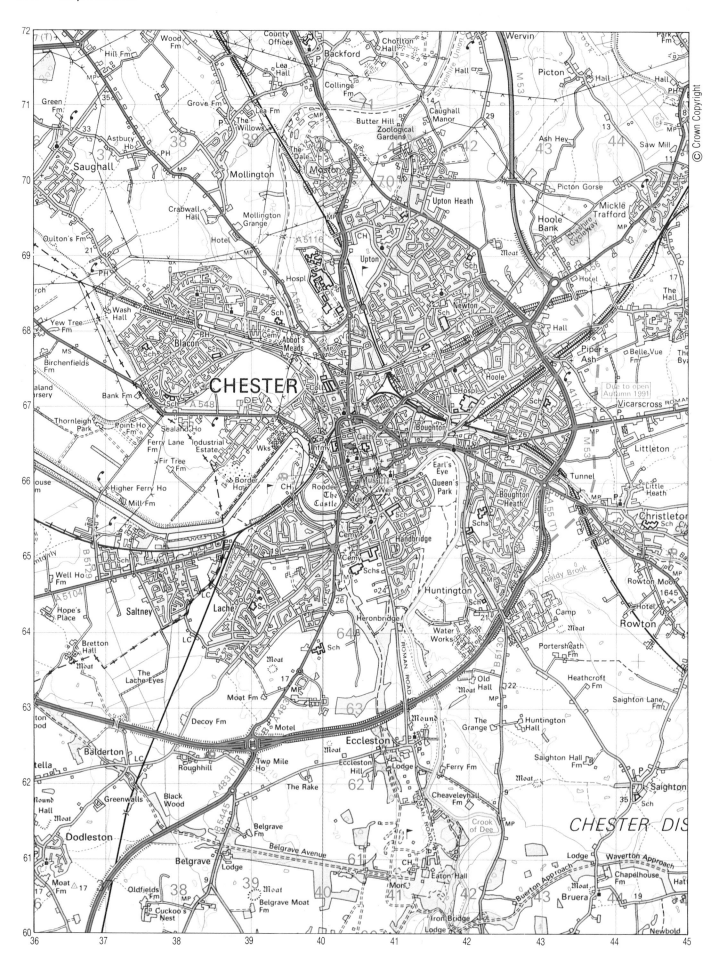

1:50 000

ROADS AND PATHS
Not necessarily rights of way

Service area M 56	Elevated
Junction number 12	En Viaduc überhöht

VOIES DE COMMUNICATIONS
VERKEHRSNETZ

Motorway (dual carriageway)
Autoroute (chaussées séparées) avec aire de service et échangeur avec numéro de l'échangeur
Autobahn (zweibahnig) mit Versorgungs- und Anschlusstelle sowie Nummer der Anschlusstelle

M 53

Motorway under construction
Autoroute en construction
Autobahn im Bau

Unfenced	Footbridge
A 41 (T)	Passerelle Fussgängerbrücke
Sans clôture	Dual carriageway
A 483	Chaussées séparées Zweibahnig

Trunk road
Route de grande circulation
Fernverkehrsstrasse

Main road
Route principale
Hauptstrasse

Main road under construction
Route principale en construction
Hauptstrasse im Bau

Uneingehegt
B 5132

Secondary road
Route secondaire
Nebenstrasse

A 855   B 885

Narrow road with passing places
Route étroite avec voies de dépassement
Enge Strasse mit Ausweich-Überholstellen

Bridge
Pont
Brücke

Road generally more than 4 m wide
Route généralement de plus de 4 m de largeur
Strasse, Minimalbreite im allg. 4 m

Road generally less than 4 m wide
Route généralement de moins de 4 m de largeur
Strasse, Maximalbreite im allg. 4 m

Other road, drive or track
Autre route, allée ou sentier
Sonstige Strasse, Zufahrt oder Feldweg

Path   Sentier   Fussweg

Gradient : 1 in 5 and steeper   1 in 7 to 1 in 5
Pente : 20% et plus   de 14% à 20%
Steigungen : 20% und mehr   14% bis 20%

Gates	Road tunnel
Barrières	Tunnel routier
Schranken	Strassentunnel

Ferry P	Ferry V

Ferry (passenger)   Ferry (vehicle)
Bac pour piétons   Bac pour véhicules
Personenfähre   Autofähre

PUBLIC RIGHTS OF WAY
(Not applicable to Scotland)

.... Footpath
━━━━━━━ Bridleway
-·-·-·-·- Road used as a public path
-+-+-+-+- Byway open to all traffic

TOURIST INFORMATION

RENSEIGNEMENTS TOURISTIQUES DIVERS
ALLGEMEINE TOURISTENANGABEN

🛈 Information centre
Bureau d'information
Informationsbüro

Selected places of tourist interest
Endroits d'un intérêt touristique particulier
Ausgesuchte Orte, von Interesse für Touristen

P Parking
Parking
Parkplatz

📞 Telephone, public/motoring organisation
Téléphone, publique/associations automobiles
Telefon, öffentliches/Automobilklub

✕ Picnic site
Emplacement de pique-nique
Picknickplatz

🏌 Golf course or links
Terrain de golf
Golfplatz

Viewpoint
Point de vue
Aussichtspunkt

PC Public convenience (in rural areas)
WC (à la campagne)
Toiletten in ländlichen Gebieten

⚑ Camp site
Terrain de camping
Campingplatz

Caravan site
Terrain pour caravanes
Wohnwagenplatz

ROUTE OF
OFFA'S DYKE PATH

▲ Youth hostel
Auberge de jeunesse
Jugendherberge

• WREXHAM

• Ruabon

National trail
Sentier de randonnée national
Nationaler Wanderweg

Offa's Dyke Path (OD Path)

RAILWAYS

━━━━	Track multiple or single		Freight line, siding or tramway
━━━━	Track narrow gauge	⊙ a ⊙ b	Station (a) principal (b) closed to passengers
━┿━	Bridges, Footbridge		Level crossing
━▦━	Tunnel		Embankment
━▦━	Viaduct		Cutting

WATER FEATURES

Marsh or salting
Towpath   Lock   Slopes   Cliff   High water mark
Aqueduct   Canal   Ford   Low water mark
Weir   Normal tidal limit   Flat rock   Lighthouse (in use)
Lake   Bridge   Sand   Beacon
Footbridge   Dunes
Canal (dry)   Mud   Lighthouse (disused)   Shingle

HEIGHTS

━50━ Contours are at 10 metres vertical interval

•144 Heights are to the nearest metre above mean sea level

ROCK FEATURES

outcrop
cliff
scree

© Crown Copyright

GENERAL FEATURES

Electricity transmission line (with pylons spaced conventionally)   Quarry

Pipe line (arrow indicates direction of flow)   Spoil heap, refuse tip or dump

ruin   Buildings   Radio or TV mast

Public buildings (selected)   Church or Chapel with tower

Bus or coach station   with spire

Coniferous wood   without tower or spire

Non-coniferous wood   Chimney or tower

Mixed wood   Glasshouse

Orchard   Graticule intersection at 5' intervals

Park or ornamental grounds   Heliport

Triangulation pillar

Windmill with or without sails

Windpump

BOUNDARIES

-·-+-·- National
-·-·-·- London Borough
National Park or Forest Park
NT National Trust

———— County, Region or Islands Area
-+-+-+- District
NT open access
NT limited access

ABBREVIATIONS

P	Post office	CH	Clubhouse
PH	Public house	PC	Public convenience (in rural areas)
MS	Milestone	TH	Town Hall, Guildhall or equivalent
MP	Milepost	CG	Coastguard

ANTIQUITIES

VILLA	Roman	⚔	Battlefield (with date)
Castle	Non-Roman	☆ Tumulus	+ Position of antiquity which cannot be drawn to scale

𝕸 Ancient Monuments and Historic Buildings in the care of the Secretaries of State for the Environment, for Scotland and for Wales and that are open to the public

The revision date of archaeological information varies over the sheet

---

1:25 000

ROADS AND PATHS
Not necessarily rights of way

		Unfenced roads and tracks are shown by pecked lines
M 1 or A 6(M)	Motorway	
A 3 (T)	Trunk road	
A 35	Main road	
B 3074	Secondary road	
A 35	Dual carriageway	
	Road generally more than 14ft wide	
	Road generally less than 14ft wide	
	Road generally less than 14ft wide, untarred	
	Other road, drive or track	
	Path	

RAILWAYS

Multiple track } Standard gauge
Single track
Narrow gauge
Siding
Cutting
Embankment
Tunnel
Road over & under
Level crossing, station

PUBLIC RIGHTS OF WAY (Not applicable to Scotland)

----------- Public paths { Footpath / Bridleway
-·-·-·- Road used as a public path

Information not available in uncoloured areas

DANGER AREA —
MOD ranges in the area
Danger!
Observe warning notices

Public rights of way indicated by these symbols have been derived from Definitive Maps as amended by later enactments or instruments held by Ordnance Survey on 1st Oct 1981 and are shown subject to the limitations imposed by the scale of mapping
The representation on this map of any other road, track or path is no evidence of the existence of a right of way

BOUNDARIES
As notified to 1-2-73

———— Geographical County
- - - - - Administrative County, County Borough or County of City
-·-·-·- London Borough
·-·-·-· Municipal Borough, Urban or Rural District, Burgh or District Council
.... Civil Parish*
-·-·-·- Borough, Burgh or County Constituency

Coincident boundaries are shown by the first appropriate symbol opposite

*Shown alternately when coincident with other boundaries

SYMBOLS

⛪	Church or chapel	with tower	VILLA	Roman antiquity (AD 43 to AD 420)	Water
		with spire	Castle	Other antiquities	
+		without tower or spire	✛	Site of antiquity	Sand, sand & shingle
Y	Glasshouse, Youth hostel		⚔ 1066	Site of battle (with date)	Mud
⊸	Bus or coach station			Gravel, sand pit	Dunes
⚓	Lighthouse, lightship, beacon			Disused pit or quarry	National Trust always open
△	Triangulation station			Chalk pit, clay pit or quarry	National Trust opening restricted
	Triangulation point on	church, chapel, lighthouse, beacon, building & chimney		Refuse or slag heap	NT National Trust for Scotland
BP, BS	Boundary Post, Stone			Sloping masonry	Electricity transmission line
T, A, R	Telephone, public, AA, RAC			Well, Spring	pylon pole
P, ·MP, MS	Post office, Mile Post, Stone				

VEGETATION
Limits of vegetation are defined by positioning of the symbols but may be delineated also by pecks or dots

	Coniferous trees	Scrub		Reeds
	Non-coniferous trees	Bracken, rough grassland	Shown collectively as rough grassland on some sheets	
	Coppice	In some areas bracken (-) and rough grassland (···) are shown separately		Marsh
	Orchard			Saltings
	Heath			

HEIGHTS AND ROCK FEATURES

50 ·   Determined by { ground survey
285 ·   { air survey

Surface heights are to the nearest foot above mean sea level. Heights shown close to a triangulation pillar refer to the station height at ground level and not necessarily to the summit

Vertical face

Loose rock   Boulders   Outcrop   Scree

Contours are at 5 metres vertical interval